THE GRIPES OF WRATH

THE GRIPES OF WRATH

Modern-day absurdities guaranteed
to make your blood boil

SIMON CARR

PIATKUS

First published in Great Britain in 2005 by Portrait
This updated paperback edition published in 2010 by Piatkus

ISBN 978-0-7499-4085-0

Text design by Andy Summers, Planet Creative
Typeset in Melior by Phoenix Photosetting, Chatham, Kent
Illustrations by Simon Pearsall
Printed and bound in Great Britain by CPI Mackays, Chatham ME5 8TD

Papers used by Piatkus are natural, renewable and recyclable
products sourced from well-managed forests and certified
in accordance with the rules of the Forest Stewardship Council.

Piatkus
An imprint of
Little, Brown Book Group
100 Victoria Embankment
London EC4Y 0DY

An Hachette UK Company
www.hachette.co.uk

www.piatkus.co.uk

Contents

Introduction   1

1   We Are Where We Are   9

2   'My Single Most Important Priority is the Safety of the British People.'   16

3   It's Amazing We Can Keep So Cheerful   34

4   I'm Sorry, That Has Been Deemed Offensive   39

5   The Happiest Days of Our Lives   45

6   Fundamentally Right   55

7   Education³   65

8   'We Just Want to Make the World a Better Place'   74

9   World-Class Public Services   90

10   It All Depends How You Look at It   106

11   That's Fair!   117

12   We Want to Re-engage Ordinary People in Politics   124

13   Our Glorious Leaders   132

14   We're Just Trying to Make Things Better   150

15   The Administrative Terror   159

16   War   175

17   I Got My Rights! (I Got Yours, Too!)   187

18   Fruit, Nuts and Other Annoyances   192

19   EU   198

Introduction

When I came back to England at the end of the Nineties, I found the country had changed enormously in the ten years I'd been away. In the ten years from the first edition of *The Gripes of Wrath*, it's changed again by almost as much. Whatever is happening to Britain, it's happening more and more quickly.

And what is it, exactly, this accelerating change? That's impossible to say, entirely. But the following are indisputably new. Milk containers now have two lids, for safety's sake. My son got an A star in his French having started French only that year. Trial by jury has been abolished in immigration cases. If a certain annoying woman in the Midlands opens the door in her underwear one more time – she can be jailed for it. The term 'brain storming' is discouraged in some quarters as it has the potential to offend epileptics. In some business sectors, salacious conversation can be penalised more fiercely than at the height of Victorian prudery.

But first, reasons to be cheerful. England seemed a happier place than when I'd left. It was more relaxed, at ease with itself, confident. Friendlier, even. We paused in front of an Underground map, my boys and I, and a Londoner stopped to ask if we needed any help. Nothing had prepared me for that, certainly not ten years of living in London in the 1980s.

More importantly, there appeared to be less snobbery in the air. People had stopped winching their accents up to pretend they belonged to a slightly higher class. Hundreds of years of English snootiness had imploded and self-destructed. Quite suddenly it seemed to me, British management weren't spending the first ten minutes of a business meeting wondering whether the other side of the desk had been to a better or a worse school than they had.

The widely derided political correctness had achieved another victory. Britons inside the magic circle where power, wealth and influence were traded had suddenly become more polite to people on the outside – in public, at least. The regions had risen in importance; regional capitals were regenerating. Girls were decisively outperforming boys in school. And those in authority behaved – or realised they had to behave – much more decently to ethnic minorities. In the middle class, the word 'nigger' had become more feared than the word 'toilet'. It had been the other way round just ten years before. That was an advance. That was an example of moral evolution.

So what am I complaining about?

In the first week back in Britain, I got on a train to go to London; when I presented my cheap day return the

2

inspector told me it wasn't valid. Cheap day returns weren't valid before 9 a.m.

'But it isn't before 9 a.m,' I said.

'This is the 8.58,' the inspector said, 'cheap day returns aren't valid before 9 a.m.'

'But it's 9.15.'

'The train is deemed to have left on time,' he said.

Now, there are legitimate ways of expressing the train company's policy but this wasn't one of them. The word 'deemed' is a giveaway. Anything that is 'deemed', in my experience, is rotten. In the old days, South African cape coloureds might be deemed to be white for some wretched political purpose or other. Now we are hearing the word more and more. Hospital trolleys are deemed to be beds, in order to fiddle hospital statistics. Buses may be deemed to be trains in order to fiddle transport statistics. Trains that are five minutes late are deemed to have arrived on time. If a country votes 'no' in a referendum they may be deemed to have given provisional approval until the government can organise another referendum. Ministers are deemed to be a very particular legal entity to take them out of the scope of the corporate manslaughter legislation. At some times these things matter more than at others. Saddam Hussein, for instance, was deemed to have weapons of mass destruction.

How dangerous is this? It's too early to tell. Maybe it always will be too early to tell. Because our activities are increasing exponentially. Everything's getting bigger, faster. Companies have to find economies of scale or they are extinguished. As systems get larger they have to be more and more idiot-proof and that makes the people who operate them more and more idiotic. In a big system the target is zero defects. That means zero discretion (it's why the train was deemed to have left on time).

Add to this the fact that the state is starting to act like an individual (a nosy neighbour or a selfless charity worker depending on your point of view). In the old days, the state used to set the rules and stand back to let people get on with their lives. That's changing. The state is in every nook and cranny of our lives telling us how much fruit we should eat (five a day, of course), how big the teddy bears should be as fairground prizes, whether children should wear gloves when feeding their pets. If we have regular contact with other people's children – even to drive them to school in a car pool – we need to be licensed by the state.

Can these confusions hurt? Oh yes, oh yes. When the state goes wrong the scale of the mistake is of a different order to those made by private companies. Our very large companies in Britain make £10 billion a year. The government takes in about £600 billion a year. When companies make fatal errors they go bankrupt and disappear. When states make mistakes there is no upper limit on the carnage possible.

Here are some changes that have either happened or are in the pipeline.

- Changing the radio station in a moving car is defined as driving without due care and attention. The correct procedure is to pull over into a designated lay-by to change stations.

- Tapping the ash of a cigarette out of a car window is defined as littering.
- Public servants shall not be allowed to help the public in emergency situations unless they have been authorised. They shall not be authorised unless they have attended appropriate training courses and been licensed by their employer. Any public servant putting him- or herself at risk in emergency circumstances without the appropriate licence shall be subject to disciplinary procedures.
- All cars shall have their headlights on when being driven.
- The police will investigate your burglary only if you can make a co-payment to the police.
- Football shall be banned in playgrounds for fear of encouraging violent behaviour patterns.
- The GPS device in your car to monitor mileage shall be modified to send details of speed-limit infractions to the penalty-notice-issuing authority.
- Boys making drawings with violent content shall be entered into a psychological evaluation programme leading to remedial treatment, if deemed necessary. (NB: representations of guns and military equipment shall be deemed violent.)
- You may be arrested for carrying a copy of Wilfred Owen's antiwar poetry in Whitehall without the permission of the Commissioner of Police. Charges may be brought under the Serious Organised Crime Act and the Prevention of Terrorism Act.
- Torture shall be allowable in certain circumstances under the Prevention of Terrorism Act, but only by officials licensed by the Health and Safety Executive guidelines.

- Joggers exercising on public pavements shall wear helmets. If jogging after dark they shall carry illumination to prevent accidents.
- Three people singing in a pub without a licence shall be subject to criminal proceedings.
- Vicars will have to attend a course on working at height if their pulpits have more than seven steps.

And so the political process reaches further down into our professional, our personal and even our private relationships.

I've been sitting up in the press gallery of parliament for ten years watching what they care to show us. Why things happen is still a mystery to me. But the mood of the government has changed dramatically. When New Labour first came to power it was all minimum wage and freedom of information; by the time they left it was all ID cards, ASBOs, police powers and security. Does it affect us personally? Well, you may be surprised. Already, under the Prevention of Terrorism Act a very surprising number of officials (some down at council level) have the power to track your Internet records. Have you been visiting any peculiar sites? Do you want the chair of your local planning committee to know about your most personal interests? It's my axiom that no person's Internet history bears public scrutiny.

Of course, our leaders are the good guys. Aren't they? Let's not argue about that now. But the political class has a marvellous array of powers available to it if it ever wants to clamp down on us, in the name of safety, security, the prevention of terrorism – and saving money. Powers of curfew, of arrest, of detention. The presumption of innocence has been eroded, expensive jury trials are on the way out, 'preventative justice' means you can be arrested and detained indefinitely without having committed an offence and without having had any trial let alone a jury trial.

All that's happened in the last five to ten years. There's more to come, of course. That's what this book is about. What we have here in these kaleidoscopic glimpses of this, that, and the other . . . is the future. It's all to come, and my bet is that it's going to be more like this rather than less like this.

1

We Are Where We Are

A marshal supervising a canoe race in the west of England stood at a hazardous river bend warning competitors not to overtake. One pair of teenagers ignored the warning, overtook, came to grief, sued the marshal for negligence and won. The judge ruled that he should have taken into account the fact that young people would ignore him.

A perfectly reasonable Bill to prevent this sort of thing was talked out of Parliament by a Labour MP (and personal injury lawyer), who said it was 'an unlimited charter to injure, kill and maim young people'.

~

While feeding their pets, some schoolchildren are required by their teachers to wear gloves. 'Health and safety' is cited as the reason. The Health and Safety Executive describe such behaviour as 'absurd' – but they have no power to stop it.

To those who hath, more shall be given

A nursery school teacher defended her class against a machete-wielding assailant; she received injuries requiring several hundred stitches and compensation of £80,000.

A woman police constable was held back from promotion on account of her gender and was compensated in the sum of £500,000.

A female merchant banker who was told she had 'nice waps' by her employer received £1.2 million.

~

Having served 37 years for a crime they did not commit, two prisoners in England were released in 2004 and awarded £350,000 compensation. But £62,000 was held back to pay for their board and lodging while they were in prison.

~

A woman in Highmoor Cross, Oxfordshire, called the police after an intruder stabbed her sister to death and inflicted a life-threatening wound on herself before fleeing. Neighbours who were tending the wounded woman begged the police to allow the ambulance to come and collect the woman. The police officer in charge of the operation refused to allow the paramedics or his own police officers into the house in case the assailant was still inside. He reasoned that the assailant might be forcing those present to plead for help in order to lure police officers into a trap. The rules would not allow him to put his officers at risk. The woman bled to death over the course of 64 minutes.

~

Labour minister John Denham was told that police officers could face disciplinary charges for saying 'nitty-gritty' because it dates from the slavery era.

~

A businessman wrote a letter objecting to a travellers' planning application. It had in it the phrase 'it's the "do as you likey" attitude that I am against'. Officers came to his house and arrested him, and held him in police cells. A council spokesman said, 'As far as we were concerned it was an offensive comment, so we got in touch with the police.' ('Likey' rhymes with 'pikey', which is a derogatory term for travellers.)

~

In the 2007 Programme for International Student Assessment (PISA) tables, Britain had fallen down the international league tables from seventh to 17th place in reading and from eighth to 24th in maths (both for 15-year-olds).

In the reading standards for five to ten-year-olds, we went from third to 19th place. The Boston survey showed our children feel less safe in school than children in Iran, Russia and Morocco.

A minister defended the results, saying we were 'average' and that our students had 'strong attitudes towards the importance of mathematics and English'. The department said, 'The UK was in the group of "higher-achieving" countries.'

~

Platform announcement: 'We apologise for the lateness of the train approaching platform one. This is due to delays.'

✿

To improve train punctuality, services have been cancelled. Punctuality is improving, but the definition of 'punctual' has been changed to include trains that don't arrive on time.

✿

A farmer trying to prevent gypsies from illegally entering his land, called the police and was immediately arrested. His presence was deemed to be liable to cause a breach of the peace.

✿

Three hospital workers made a citizen's arrest on a thief, and sat on him while waiting for the police. The security guards required the citizens to let him up, fearing the thief could sue the hospital if he was hurt on the premises. The thief was allowed to sit on a wall. Then he ran away.

✿

A dyslexic bus driver won a discrimination claim against Stagecoach because he couldn't read the bus timetable.

✿

Sue Bright of the Women's Institute was barred from giving homemade cakes to Essex hospital patients because Health and Safety inspectors were unable to check the hygiene standards in her kitchen. At the same time, hospital-acquired infections caused by defective hygiene killed between 5,000 and 20,000 people in hospitals that actually were inspected by Health and Safety officials.

Around 50,000 cases of *Clostridium difficile* are reported from hospitals every year.

A related fact may be that the number of full-time cleaning posts halved between 1986 and 2004. A Freedom of Information request to 377 hospitals in 2007 showed half of them had 'poor cleanliness'.

～

A friend of mine is a disability officer in an educational institution. She has to arrange meetings with old-age pensioners, a dozen of them at a time.

One old lady stood up in her induction group and announced that she was allergic to wasps, and if she was stung she would die unless she was injected with the serum (which she produced in one hand) via a hypodermic (in her other hand).

My friend was obliged to point out that if she were stung by a wasp no one would be allowed to inject her. If the old lady died, anyone physically involved could be sued for compensation by any surviving relatives. It was legally possible for others to help the old lady 'into the recovery position', and they could help her to inject herself. But to take control of the hypodermic without a current qualification would render the helper liable for civil suit.

The proper procedure was to put her in the recovery position, phone for qualified help, and watch her die.

～

The Institute of Occupational Safety and Health, representing 36,000 Health and Safety experts, warned its members about the legal danger of public footpaths: 'When clearing snow and ice, it is probably worth stopping at the boundaries of the property under your control.'

Why? Clearing a public path 'can lead to an action for damages against the company, e.g. if members of the public, assuming that the area is still clear of ice and thus safe to walk on, slip and injure themselves'.

John McQuater, president of the Association of Personal Injury Lawyers, confirmed this: 'If you do nothing you cannot be liable. If you do something, you could be liable to a legal action.'

'My Single Most Important Priority is the Safety of the British People.'

The Metropolitan police were charged with safety breaches after two officers fell through roofs while chasing burglars (the case failed, in the end).

In Blackburn, school pupils were banned from picking up litter in case it contained broken glass, needles or dog faeces. A nearby council has banned backstroke in the pools to prevent collisions.

A head teacher banned rugby and footballs in the playground because two pupils were hit by them in the lunchbreak. She said, 'Parents are much more litigious these days.'

In Bognor Regis, children have been required to wear hard hats to ride beach donkeys.

In Norwich, councillors threatened to cut down horse chestnut trees to prevent children being hurt by conkers.

Girl Guides were sued by a family whose teenage daughter was hurt by spitting fat when she was cooking sausages (inadequate supervision: £5,000).

A swing under a chestnut tree in Sheet, Hampshire was removed after councillors said, 'Someone will fall, they will get hurt, we will get sued and we're not insured.'

~

'My wife was at work when she received the chilling call from the nursery: our two-year-old son Jim had had an accident,' wrote Ian Evans in *The Times*. 'She grabbed her bag and keys, ready to drive to the nearest hospital. In fact he'd only grazed his knee; the nursery nurse was seeking permission to put a plaster on, then passed the phone to her supervisor to confirm that the OK had been given. A one-off, you might think, but in fact this is not untypical in the all-caring, all-smothering – and paranoid – world of nursery schools.'

And from the same article:

Emma Bracewell, in Suffolk, was told not to bring in egg boxes to her sons' nursery. 'They said it was because of fears over salmonella – from the boxes.'

Kiran Jones, in Bromley, southeast London, discovered that his nursery wouldn't administer Calpol to his nine-month-old because he hadn't left a spoon.

Laurent Lucas, a former nursery worker, explains: 'We live in a society where people often sue for 'negligence'. I have had parents complaining because their child had an allergic reaction to a plaster.'

~

Guidelines issued by Derby City Council tell teachers who plan to lead students on summer trips that they should consider keeping a supply of maximum-factor sun cream to spray onto pupils, although they should not rub it in for fear of being accused of inappropriate contact.

In Bristol, staff at Hillcrest Primary School confiscated a bottle of Factor 60 sunblock that an eight-year-old boy had brought to school, because it was forbidden for students to possess medication, according to the BBC News website. If the child was easily sunburned, he should have worn a long-sleeved shirt and sun hat. Offering the simplest solution to safety problems, the council suggested that educators consider cancelling field outings entirely on days that are too sunny.

Be prepared!

A Scout group from the Manchester area was eating their picnic lunch before undertaking a guided tour of the Gaping Ghyll cave. One of the Scouts noticed a small cave across a stream and asked the Scout leader for permission to explore it. The leader refused permission, pointing out that the cave could be dangerous and that they had neither the equipment nor the expertise to explore it. The Scout was accompanied by his father, who had been encouraged to join the group. The Scout went out of earshot of the leader and said to his father that he wanted to go into the cave. His father agreed, provided his son with a cigarette lighter and accompanied him into the cave, where the child plunged over a precipice to his death.

The judge declared the Scout leader negligent. He should have assumed that the father would not understand risks in the countryside, coming, as he had, from an urban centre, and that he failed to prevent the father taking his son into the cave, by force if necessary.

~

'A Scout campsite had created a water slide on a gentle slope by laying a length of heavy-duty polythene on the ground, which was then covered with soapy water. The supervising adults explained that people should not run and dive onto the sheet but that they should simply sit at the top. For safety, the participants were provided with lightweight, plastic canoeing helmets and were instructed to fasten these securely before descending. A youth leader with a party of non-Scout children decided to have a go. He selected a helmet without reference to the supervising Scout leaders (who were checking that the helmets were secure) and dived headlong down the slope. The loosely fitted helmet struck the ground and the front slipped down cutting the bridge of his nose. This was a relatively minor injury. However, a claim was brought and the matter proceeded to trial. The Scouts lost and the Judge held that the Scout leaders should have ensured that people could not get on to the slide without the helmets being checked.'

Joseph Morrison v. *The Scout Association*

~

In 2005, a government minister was present at the scene of a drive-by shooting on an inner-city estate in London. 'He was in incredible agony, screaming in pain, drifting in and out of consciousness,' the minister, David Lammy, said. While the youth was bleeding, ambulances arrived with police cars and parked 200 yards away from the boy and did not approach him for another 12 minutes while a risk assessment was carried out.

Mr Lammy made angry announcements that this was entirely unacceptable and would see the practice changed. When I ran into him a couple of years later in the Commons I asked him what changes he'd brought in. 'It's more complicated than I thought,' he said, and smiled ruefully.

~

An American student recalls the briefing given to her class when she was studying in London. A policewoman asked the females if they were carrying Mace. 'Three girls raised their hands. She told us we couldn't use it, shouldn't even carry it, it was illegal.

'Then she instructed us on how properly to be a victim. If we were attacked, we were to assume a defensive posture, such as raising our hands to block an attack. The reason (and she spelled it out in no uncertain terms) was that if a witness saw the incident and we were to attempt to defend ourselves by fighting back, the witness would be unable to tell who the aggressor was. However, if we rolled up in a ball, it would be clear who the victim was.'

WARNING LABELS

Lawsuits, and fear of lawsuits, have prompted manufacturers to issue warnings against even obvious misuses of consumer products.

A label on a snow sled warns **'Beware: sled may develop high speed under certain snow conditions.'**

A 12-inch-high storage rack for compact disks warns **'Do not use as a ladder.'**

A 5-inch fishing lure, which sports three steel hooks, cautions users that it is **'Harmful if swallowed.'**

A smoke detector warns **'Do not use the silence feature in emergency situations. It will not extinguish a fire.'**

From *Michigan Lawsuit Abuse Watch* (www.mlaw.org)

Sudan 1, a cancer-causing food dye according to media at the time, resulted in 400 lines of foods being withdrawn from supermarkets early in 2005. It was particularly known for giving a kick to Cross and Blackwell's Worcester sauce. The *Sunday Telegraph* reported that to ingest Sudan 1 in the amounts that were shown to cause harm in rats, a human would have to consume the sauce at the rate of three tons every day for two years.

Walk this talk

Organisers of the annual Two Steeples Walk take walkers past a couple of churches, a canal and the tea rooms. The Leicestershire and Rutland Rural Community Council now require them to fill out a two-page risk-assessment form, which includes the following checks:

Hazards associated with task:

Traffic: Does your walk involve crossing a busy road?

Electricity: Are there any electric fences on the walk?

Weather: Would adverse weather conditions make this walk hazardous?

Water: Does your walk involve walking on a canal towpath, near a river or a lake?

Slips, trips and falls: Do you advise people on sensible footwear/clothing?

Are there likely to be any:

Rabbit holes?

Overhanging branches?

Barbed-wire fences?

Slippery surfaces when wet?

Stiles/steps that could be slippery when wet?

Buyers Beware

McDonald's Coffee

Warning – Contents may be hot.

7-Up

Contents under pressure. Cap may blow off causing eye or other serious injury. Point away from face and people, especially when opening.

Sainsbury's Mineral Water

Suitable for vegetarians.

Child-Sized Superman Costume

Wearing of this garment does not enable you to fly.

Dremel Electric Rotary Tool

This product not intended for use as a dental drill.

Wet-Nap

Directions: Tear open packet and use.

Claymore Anti-Personnel Mine

Do not eat.

Nytol Sleep Aid

Warning: May cause drowsiness.

Sainsbury's Peanuts

Warning: Contains nuts.

Bowl Fresh

Safe to use around pets and children, although it is not recommended that either be permitted to drink from toilet.

Clairol Herbal Essences Maximum Hold Hairspray

Warning: Do not smoke until hair is dry.

Harry Potter Broom

This broom does not actually fly.

Rowenta Iron

Warning: Never iron clothes on the body.

Unknown vacuum cleaner

1   Do not use to pick up gasoline or flammable liquids.
2   Do not use to pick up anything that is currently burning.

Power Puff Girls Halloween Costume

You cannot save the world!

~

Kava-kava has been the national drink of Tonga for many hundreds of years. It has been banned in Europe for reasons of health and/or safety. There is no evidence it is any more dangerous than alcohol.

~

Two police officers, 12 coastguards and a four-man lifeboat crew worked together to retrieve a £20 toy plane stranded on a cliff. A rope team abseiled down the 200-foot

Huntcliff at Saltburn, Cleveland, to retrieve it at a cost of £5,000. A spokesman for the Staithes and Runswick Lifeboat said the emergency services wanted to avoid any risk to the public who might have tried to reach the plane themselves.

～

Heavily pregnant Michelle Colley, who was in her mid-twenties, was seen screaming at a rear-bedroom window so some neighbours tried to rescue the family using a ladder and garden hose. Other neighbours who wanted to help said they were prevented from doing so by police, who feared for their safety.

Neighbour Davey Davis, 38, a plant operator, said some people were upset because police prevented them from trying to rescue the family, on safety grounds.

'Someone had got a ladder and someone else had a hose. We were trying to get in. I've never seen anything like it,' he said.

'She was screaming "get my kids out".' She was eight and a half months pregnant, due to give birth soon.

Police arrived before the fire brigade and, according to Mr Davis and other neighbours, tried to keep residents away from the blaze, saying it was too dangerous.

That caused frustration among the neighbours: 'Some people were going loopy because they wanted to get in. People were shouting at the police and everything,' he said.

Detective Superintendent Peter McGuinness said, 'I would like to commend our officers who were first on the scene.

'The Fire Brigade were only minutes away, but our officers were faced with a raging fire. They handled the incident as professionally as we would expect them to and they then worked long into the night.'

Report in *Yorkshire Post* (only the five-year-old daughter survived, as an orphan)

Occupational Safety and Health website, New Zealand

Back problems are a risk for sex workers. These, according to OSH, can be dealt with by 'ensuring that all beds and other workstations support the back and allow for a variety of services to be performed without strain or discomfort'.

Some repetitive activities, the OSH website tells us, 'cannot be avoided ... The best way to avoid overuse disorders for sex workers is to try to alternate between repetitive and non-repetitive activities. For example, repetitive massage which could cause overuse injury to the hands, arm and back could be alternated with other (non-repetitive) activities'.

'Comprehensive training in the safe use of all equipment, particularly that used in B&D and S&M fantasy work, as well as training in correct massage techniques, should be provided to workers who use these techniques.'

∿

Office workers would be better off eating lunch in a toilet – the recruitment firm Connections cited a US report showing a typical desk harboured 400 times more disease-causing bacteria than a toilet seat.

*

A banker driving down Whitehall was stopped by the police and his car searched. They found in his briefcase a Swiss Army pen knife, so he was charged with carrying a bladed weapon, arrested and kept in cells for the rest of the day.

*

While these community-service officers were making us more secure by arresting the banker, four protestors wandered through the complex security arrangements and got into the Cabinet Office, where they put on blood-soaked clothes and protested against the invasion of Iraq. They were charged with attempted burglary.

*

Philip Maugham of Terra Nova Training, a management training organisation, said his insurance premiums had gone from £1,050 a year to £5,500, but he was unable to find cover for outdoor activities. This is partly due to legislation under which insurers were required to pay the cost of any NHS fees for clients.

*

The Little Chef logo has been redesigned. 'People think he's a child and it's unsafe for him to be carrying food,' the chairman said.

*

'Rules now state that Brownie leaders are not allowed to make use of lavatory rolls to make things (in case of germs) or to rub sun cream on to a child's arm (in case of sexual abuse), or if a child is injured to take her home in their car without the presence of another adult (ditto). My friend remarked it is getting quite hard to recruit Brownie leaders.'

Charles Moore, *Spectator*

EU regulations to ensure that aflatoxin mould did not grow on nuts and dried fruit are far tougher than international standards but were estimated to prevent 1.4 deaths per billion consumers (there aren't a billion consumers in the EU).

WARNING LABELS

'Do not use for personal hygiene' (on a toilet brush)

'This product moves when used' (on a scooter)

'Once used rectally, the thermometer should not be used orally' (on a digital thermometer)

'Do not use this product as a toy, pillow or flotation device' (on a three-inch bag of air used for packaging)

From *Michigan Lawsuit Abuse Watch* (www.mlaw.org)

Of control orders

'A different process of decision making will be used from that which applies when people are arrested on the basis that they have already committed an offence. This point goes to the heart of the matter. The hon. Gentleman is talking about a justice system that examines things after they have happened, but control orders are designed to deal with not only what has happened, but what might happen.'

Hazel Blears, then Home Office Minister, *Hansard*

This means – because the safety of the British people is the first priority of the prime minister – that a British citizen can be arrested and presented to a judge without being told:

- who has accused him
- what the charge is
- what the evidence against him is, and
- without having committed an offence.

~

Reuben Powell (white, middle-aged, middle-class artist) was photographing an old print works for his reference. 'The car skidded to a halt like something out of *Starsky & Hutch* and this officer jumped out very dramatically and said "What are you doing?" I told him I was photographing the building and he said he was going to search me under the Anti-Terrorism Act.' Mr Powell was arrested, handcuffed, held and questioned for five hours.

~

Bob Patefield was taking photographs of Christmas celebrations. A police community-support officer approached him and said, 'Because of the Terrorism Act and everything in the country, we need to get everyone's details who is taking pictures of the town.'

Mr Patefield asked if there was any reason to suspect him of anything. She said, 'I believe your behaviour was quite suspicious in the manner in which you were taking photographs in the town centre ... I'm suspicious in why you were taking those pictures.'

Eventually Mr Patefield was arrested, held for eight hours and released without charge. Unlike a young Brazilian woman, Sinona Bonomo, he was not thrown to the ground, held there and handcuffed in the same sort of encounter.

The number of citizens arrested for taking photographs is not held centrally.

There's a whopping new poster and press campaign run by the Health and Safety Executive. The full-sized poster features a jogger in a multicoloured tracksuit surrounded by paparazzi flashing their cameras at him.

If you haven't seen the campaign, I invite you to imagine what caption, what explanatory text, could possibly justify the expense of the campaign. What urgent news justifies the cost of its telling?

The line on the poster reads, 'Staying active can help a bad back.' This statement falls into the category of 'true but useless', because equally true is the statement: 'Lying face down on the floor can help a bad back.' And what the hell are those cameramen doing in the picture?

The small print in the press ad tells employers to 'encourage [their] staff to stay active' if they have bad backs. And they are told 'to act early'. The sign-off line is, 'Whatever your job look after your back.'

How is this campaign to be judged and audited? What constitutes failure? You can be certain it will not be judged on whether absenteeism due to bad backs reduces. That would be a vulgar-minded, bean-counting approach.

No, they'll have to come up with some research that shows they have managed to change the cultural attitude to bad backs (it's the notorious excuse of malingerers). They'll get some compliant research company to produce data showing that 28 per cent of employers are now 'somewhat more likely or much more likely to encourage employees with bad backs to remain active'.

This is an admirable approach for fakers, whingers and malingerers – but it could be very dangerous for people who have bad backs. My own bad back gets much worse when I run (I don't run well). And then there's my blood pressure, severely worsened by this Health and Safety campaign.

Warning: safety can damage your health

'He knows he isn't going to get better physically. But what he really wants to do is to go out in the sun, to feel its warmth on his face, and to breathe fresh air. To me that seems a pretty fair request. "It's against Health and Safety," replies the ward sister, when I suggest this would be the best thing for his mood. This is the blanket reply for anything that deviates from accepted protocol.

'I wonder where the prohibition on taking sick men into the sunshine is written. But the nurse is bigger than I am so I don't push this point.

'"Well, okay, I'll take him myself, then," I offer.

'"You can't," she says. "You're not insured to push a wheelchair."

'I've come up against this one before. A number of times, while I was working in surgery, I had sick patients who needed a scan when porters weren't available, so I pushed them myself – much to the anguish of the ward sister, who failed to understand that if patients didn't get their scans they were more likely to die than to sue if I pushed them without insurance to the X-ray department.

'"I'll take full responsibility for anything that happens," pipes up Mr Hazlitt, who has been listening from inside his room.

'"No, it's against Health and Safety," comes the reply yet again. I write in the notes and leave the ward. There's nothing that can be done for Mr Hazlitt and indeed, in a few days he died.

'Officially, he never did get to go outside. But of course, the thing about Health and Safety, it can only be enforced while you're at work. I'm sure you can guess what happened, unofficially, at five minutes past five, when I wasn't officially working and the nurse was on her break.'

Max Pemberton in his *Telegraph* column
'Trust me, I'm a junior doctor'

It's Amazing We Can Keep So Cheerful

These words and phrases were taken from one day's newspaper coverage, from one newspaper.

Coward and bully boy, blood in the abdominal cavity, SATs boycott, hospital blunders, heartbroken father, Brown's ITV crony pension bonanza, MPs take home 28 times the average voter's pay, abusive text messages, channelling money to terrorists, private-jet air hostess, life-threatening head injuries ...

She is cold and nasty, glowering henchmen, globe-trotting gap-year jaunt, running scared, campaigner targeted, no more hotpants, child attacks soar, Hazel Blears, second post-mortem, life-threatening error, growing criticism from senior figures, lucrative international lecture circuit, saving Mrs Blair £6.24, You're fired!, TV porn, expenses of his own wife, secret documents on camera, proxy war ...

Deep in the bowels of Downing Street, grasping colleagues and smearing their opponents, mauled, unjustifiably roughed up, medium-sized similar horrors, long-running violence, human evil, fierce drama, fickle mob, cowardice, treachery, break their promise, smooth politician, utter despair, hopeless agony, lies, betrayal, mistrust, violence, injustice, impunity, cynical power worship, government by crude force, indefensible arrest ...

Unlovely Bob Quick, smacked down very hard, anti-terror operations are political propaganda, our worst Prime Minister, parcel of garbage, cowardly courts, bureaucratic police, doomed war, mass army of political correctness, my ID wasn't good enough, killing off the earth with all this rubbish, suspenders, landscape of wrecked and burning cars, 7.15 cattle truck to Westminster, jaded, tipsy and dizzy, head butt threat, biometric ID tests, out of control and swearing, yelling abuse, full-on assault, staring daggers, officer in G20 death probe signs off sick, desperation, pain and fear she'll never see her two boys again, dragged to court in handcuffs ...

Cut off his own fingertips, furious family fight to keep father away, fury at the factory gates, a £70,000 bungle but Post Office won't explain, Brown's attack dogs hate women, cut their outgoings to the bone, 70 letters of complaint to the lenders, cash vehicle that fell off a cliff, impossible to value or sell, beats his children with a riding crop, fascist salute, 'laughing and dancing' during Hillsborough memorial service, recently found work in a supermarket, a plea for 'less angry' Britain ...

'It's time people stopped being so darned pessimistic,' says Mandelson in cheer-up call to voters ...

~

The editor of *New Scientist* in 1975: 'The threat of a new ice age must now stand alongside nuclear war as a likely source of wholesale death and misery for mankind.'

End-of-life-as-we-know-it stories

- The world's oceans have absorbed half the carbon dioxide produced since the Industrial Revolution and are becoming more acid as a result. This threatens the existence of plankton and other tiny animals, which form the base of the food chain of the oceans and thus the existence of life on earth.

- Discarded plastics are getting into the food chain and interfering with the endocrine cycle and thus the production of sex hormones in animals. An all-female future will lead to the extinction of life on earth.

- Global warming is increasing the rainfall at the equator and thus the salinity balance of the northern oceans. This is creating a 50 per cent chance that the Gulf Stream will stop, and bring arctic weather conditions as far south as Bournemouth.

- A dangerous volcano in the Canary Islands that could send a wave as high as Nelson's Column crashing into the major population centres of America's east coast is not being closely monitored, scientists warn. Boston, New York, Washington DC and Miami would be virtually wiped off the map and tens of millions killed, said Professor Bill McGuire of the Benfield Greig Hazard Research Centre at University College London.

- Gamma-ray bursts close enough to affect life in some way occur once every five million years or so – around a thousand times since life began.

~

'Examples of bioterrorism have been very rare. The only documented terrorist use of a biological agent was in Oregon, where in 1984 a religious cult allegedly contaminated several salad bars with salmonella, with hundreds of illnesses but no deaths. The only documented terrorist uses of chemical agents were in Japan where a religious cult used sarin, a nerve gas, killing seven people in the suburb Matsumoto in 1994, and used it again in 1995 in a Tokyo subway killing 12 people and injuring many more.'

Doctors Hillel Cohen, Victor Sidel and Robert Gould,
American Journal of Public Health

I'm Sorry, That Has Been Deemed ~~Offensive~~

Ten viewers complained about a Renault car ad (showing people shaking uncontrollably as the car passed) and it was taken off air. Complainants claimed the ad mocked sufferers of Parkinson's disease.

A Home Office presentation on counterterrorism included a cartoon showing four Arabs in beards and headgear under a sign reading HUMAN BOMB CLASS. The instructor is saying, 'Pay attention, I'm only going to do this once.' Negative reaction included Anas Altikriti, who described the cartoon as, amongst other things, 'untrue'.

Oh, what a gay play!

The editor of St Andrews University student newspaper, Jo Kerr, reviewed a play called *Corpus Christi* in the following terms. It was 'a comedy portraying Jesus as a gay son of an alcoholic father ... attacked by a not-so-merry band of fundamentalist Christians from Wales. It's almost beyond belief (apart from the fact that I have secretly suspected the Welsh of evil doings ever since they spawned the caterwauling Charlotte Church).'

The paper was locked out of its offices by its landlord, the Students' Association, until the staff agreed to undergo 'diversity awareness training'. It was found to have been guilty of discrimination against minority groups (in this case, the Welsh).

*

A social worker helping Asian battered women forgot the name of an interpreter: 'It was Pamela, Popalam or Popadom – something like that,' she said. She was summoned before a disciplinary tribunal and told she could only stay in her job if she attended anti-racism lessons and wrote an essay on the Stephen Lawrence case.

*

The term 'British Isles' is said to be offensive to those in the Republic of Ireland and it is proposed to rename them as Islands of the North Atlantic (IONA).

*

A reader who tried to sign up for a web-chat with David Aaronovitch, the *Guardian*'s loyal Blairite columnist at the time, found his username – 'exlabourvoter' – rejected. 'Unfortunately, we cannot validate your account,' came the emailed explanation, 'as your username is deemed to be offensive.'

~

Bear necessities

A company that sells cuddly teddy bears through the mail has angered mental health advocates with a special item for Valentine's Day.

The Vermont Teddy Bear Co. is featuring a 15-inch bear in a straitjacket. The $69.95 stuffed animal is called the 'Crazy for You Bear' and comes with its own commitment papers.

'This bear was created in the spirit of Valentine's Day and as with all of our bears it was designed to be a lighthearted depiction of the sentiment of love,' the company said in a statement.

Mental health advocates believe the bear is 'a tasteless use of marketing that stigmatizes persons with mental illness,' said Jerry Goessel, executive director of the Vermont Chapter of the National Alliance for the Mentally Ill.

~

A couple were told they could not use a photo of their bare-chested baby son for a passport because it could upset Muslims.

Tracey Barnes said the Home Office told her, 'Your photos are not acceptable as the child appears to be unclothed ... If you were to travel to an Islamic country they might find it offensive.' The family were going to Crete in May and paid £22 for the photo. But seven-month-old Lewis was sick on his top and they took it off.

The Muslim Council of Britain said, 'The Home Office must be absurd in the extreme if they think Muslims would be offended by a naked baby.'

～

Reports came from Liverpool that the local authority was planning to ban depicting smoking on stage. Whether *Hamlet* should be renamed is not in front of the council.

～

Eighty people got a nasty flu and died in Mexico. May they rest in peace. But 200,000 of us die every day in the world, so the Mexican victims aren't exactly objects of rational fear.

The World Health Organisation has warned that the swine flu virus 'has the potential to become a pandemic'.

The director of the World Influenza Centre said of the outbreak and its future, 'It's difficult to look on the bright side.'

Actually, it is not at all difficult, with a little insensitivity. The bright side is that, compared to the predicted 20 million infections and 90,000 deaths, very few people have been affected and there have been very few deaths. We haven't had a major outbreak of flu for forty years, before 2009 there had been no swine flu in the UK for a decade, and also no one in Britain died of bird flu.

It may well be true that, virally speaking, H1 swine flu is 'already worse than H5'. But that H5N1 bird flu was hardly worth worrying us with at all. According to the World Health Organisation, 257 people have died of it in the last seven years, while the best part of a billion others have died of non-bird-flu-related causes.

Nonetheless, we were worried enough at the time. Avian flu was subjected to 'detailed modelling' by the Department of Health. It revealed 'mortality estimates of between 50,000 and 750,000 additional deaths, depending on both the attack rate and case fatality rate'. That is, in English, maybe 50,000 people would die or 750,000 people would die, depending on how many people died. In the event, nobody in Britain died.

~

When AIDS first came to prominence in the 1980s, it was widely accepted that most people would be infected over the next generation. The creation of misleading graphs, tortured tables and spurious argumentation was incredible. In the end, no one believed it. But we had to go through fifteen years without AIDS infecting most of us before we could accept it.

~

The Millennium Bug grew in a similar culture. The BBC estimated that $300 million had been spent on preventing a global computer crash that would destroy the world's processing power. After nothing happened, the organisers of the prevention drive declared it a great success. But companies – and indeed countries – that did nothing performed as well as those who had spent the $300 million.

~

And then there was the volcanic ash cloud from Iceland that paralysed air travel in 2010. The decision to close

European airspace for so long cost the airline industry $1.7 billion. The height of the cloud never reached more than 10,000 feet. Cruising altitude of passenger jets: 30,000 feet.

The Happiest Days of Our Lives

Nine million citizens are now assumed to be potential paedophiles and abusers and are required to be licensed by the state if they have regular contact with children not their own.

∼

Olive Rack, supervising one of her nursery classes, saw a two-year-old hitting a baby over the head with a toy brick. She marched the child to 'the naughty chair'. She was observed doing this by school inspectors. Despite the opinion of the two-year-old's mother, Mrs Rack was prosecuted for (and eventually acquitted of) assault.

∼

From *Georgie*, a new book for ten-year-olds, by Malachy Doyle: 'I sit on the toilet, pushing it all into my hand, and then I paint the walls brown. Brown to wash out the white of my anger. Brown to make them hate me. Oh, how they hate me.'

~

A 4-foot-tall boy of 12 tried to rob a grocery store armed with a sawn-off, doubled-barrelled shotgun. He had no previous convictions. His lawyer said, 'Since the offence his behaviour has been exemplary.'

~

My friend is a good mother. She does her son's coursework for him, and keeps his marks high. Her friend is an even better mother. Her useless son was about to be thrown out of a top university unless his next essay was up to the mark. He told her about it the night before it was due in. She went and slept on the floor of his room at the college in order to work all night writing it. And, yes, it was good enough to get him another year at the university.

But two things. First, doesn't this ambition push the children out of their depth? And, second, what about the boys who don't have mothers like this?

~

Cherilyn Lloyd Jones, a food-technology teacher at Brecon High School, says, 'We spend a lot of time on HACCP [Hazard Analysis and Critical Control Points]. Instead of learning how to make biscuits, pupils are taught how to identify the moments in biscuit manufacture when microbes are most likely to multiply.'

Secondary school

Female teachers	251,000
Male teachers	113,300

Primary school

Female teachers	142,000
Male teachers	26,000

'Fed up' with Christmas, a girl without a licence or insurance and with twice the legal limit of alcohol in her bloodstream took her father's Vauxhall Corsa to drive the 30 miles to Berkshire to see her friends. After numerous collisions with the kerb she was arrested for drink-driving. She was twelve.

In the Congressional Testimony of Terrance Woodworth, a deputy director of the Drug Enforcement Administration, the number of prescriptions written for Ritalin (the drug prescribed for children deemed to be hyperactive) went up by a multiple of five in the US between 1991 and 2002.

Ritalin prescriptions in 2002: 250,000.

Ritalin prescriptions in 2007: 535,000.

Aye, aye, kick ass cap'n

A modern, confident 12-year-old girl walks into the kitchen and tells her mother to make her some toast. The mother says, 'There is the bread and there is the toaster' – and the 12-year-old girl flashes back furiously, 'I'm not your slave!'

$\sim$

'How would Richmal Compton's William Brown have fared if he had filled in the Home Office questionnaire (it led to headlines saying, "One in four boys are criminals")? Admitting to just six minor crimes – a playground bundle, a skipped bus fare or a shop-lifted chocolate bar – would have dubbed William a "serious or prolific offender". Tying oily Herbert Lane to a tree, shooting at birds with his bow and arrow, fraudulently obtaining cake by impersonating someone's nephew – that is three already. But William already owns a clasp knife, and possessing a dangerous weapon is a serious crime. The survey only required one of those to categorise William as a criminal.'

Janice Turner, *The Times*

$\sim$

One in four children leave primary school at eleven unable to read, write or count to required levels.

$\sim$

In 2008 the Royal Society of Chemistry said pupils are trained to answer 'undemanding questions to satisfy the needs of league tables and national targets'. They said that the record-breaking exam results were 'illusory'.

In the same year, 53 per cent of pupils failed to achieve five A to C grade GCSEs including English and Maths. The department said, 'Standards in science have improved year on year.'

About 15 per cent of sixteen-year-olds in 2008 finished school without achieving a single satisfactory GCSE (that is, grade C or above) in any subject. Ministers said there had been 'a sustained improvement'.

~

In independent schools, 30 per cent of pupils get three As at A level. In state schools, the figure is 8 per cent.

~

Sociology professor Frank Furedi says he is forbidden to photograph his son playing football unless he gets the permission of every parent on the field.

'This is next to impossible,' he writes on his website. 'So basically it means I don't have a pictorial memory of my child doing athletics and football, which to me is a symptom of the fact we're all looking at the world from the point of view of the pedophile. We think every adult is a potential pedophile, and ultimately that's a triumph of pedophilia over common sense.'

~

London mayor Boris Johnson reports a BA stewardess asking him to move his seat as he is sitting next to children. It is BA policy not to allow men to sit next to children.

~

Gas engineers working downstairs are not allowed to be left in a house with a fifteen-year-old sleeping upstairs in his or her bed.

~

Governments have told us that getting a suntan is the first step towards skin cancer and as a result adopted sun prevention standards from Australia. Now Dr Brian Diffey of Newcastle General Hospital says one in ten children in Britain don't get enough sun to manufacture Vitamin D. Among teenage boys this figure rises to 42 per cent.

Children all over the world were polled on their favourite activity. 'Going to school' was nominated favourite by:

- 18 per cent of Americans
- 28 per cent of Japanese
- 36 per cent of Chinese

Remaking history

A third of all 15–34-year-olds were unaware that the Battle of Britain took place in World War Two.

Fifteen per cent of 16–24-year-olds thought that when Orangemen march on 12 July they are celebrating the victory at Helm's Deep. The battle actually occurs at the end of The Two Towers, the second book of Tolkien's trilogy The Lord of the Rings.

Five per cent of the same age group questioned in a BBC poll thought the defeat of the Spanish Armada was masterminded by Gandalf.

'Writing in the *Daily Mail*, David Bellamy asserted that "the link between the burning of fossil fuel and global warming is a myth". Like almost all the climate change deniers, he based his claim on a petition produced in 1998 by the Oregon Institute of Science and Medicine and "signed by over 18,000 scientists". Had Bellamy studied the signatures, he would have discovered that the "scientists" included Ginger Spice and the cast of *M*A*S*H*. The Oregon Institute is run by a fundamentalist Christian called Arthur Robinson ...

Anyone could sign the petition and anyone did; only a handful of the signatories are experts in climatology ... And yet, six years later, this petition is still being wheeled out to suggest that climatologists say global warming isn't happening.'

George Monbiot, *Guardian*

The University of East Anglia climate fiasco has caused some in the laity to go back reaching for their brains. But the problem isn't science: it's politics.

There was the refusal of information requests. The tricks to shaft opponents. The plan to de-register an academic journal that had gone to the other side. The impulse to destroy files rather than let them fall into the wrong hands. The refusal to share primary data ... We get that all the time in Parliament.

And it fitted in with the communications strategy first leaked in the 1990s – the climatologists' plan was to spread global-warming panic as a spur to action. But, as soon as the scientists adopted a public purpose, they moved along the spectrum from academics to activists to lobbyists to political.

They're very important, these East Anglians. They are in charge of datasets that underlie the 'settled science' of the multitrillion-dollar global-warming movement.

And, boy, have they caught up with the lessons from the last decade of public administration! The text below was written by the programmer processing the data at the university.

... the expected 1990–2003 period is MISSING – so the correlations aren't so hot! Yet the WMO codes and station names/locations are identical (or close). What the hell is supposed to happen here? Oh yeah – there is no 'supposed', I can make it up. So I have ...

'Reconstruction is based on tree-ring density records. NOTE: recent decline in tree-ring density has been ARTIFICIALLY REMOVED to facilitate calibration. THEREFORE, post-1960 values will be much closer to observed temperatures than they should be, which will incorrectly imply the reconstruction is more skilful than it actually is ...

... we know the file starts at yr 440, but we want nothing till 1400

So now we have to add climate scientists to the list of professionals who treat us as hawks treat chicks. The them-and-us is getting more pronounced. We're all drifting apart from each other – it's not to do with social equality but sectional interests, the triumph of the political class, and professional tribalism as they extract their fees and levies and taxes from us with such impunity.

NB: Mind you, for all their trickery the East Anglians might still be right. The pro-vaccine lobby in the mid-nineteenth century falsified their data like billy-o.

~

The number of people believing climate change is an established fact fell from 41 per cent in 2009 to 26 per cent in the first half of 2010.

~

'Remind yourself that tantrums are a measure of intimacy. Children usually reserve tantrums for the most trusted, safe people in their lives – their parents. The next time your child is having a tantrum, remind yourself that you're being chosen because your child feels close to you.'

Laura Davis, Janis Keyser,
Becoming the Parent You Want to Be

Fundamentally Right

'Hate crime is an iceberg which is 90 per cent invisible. And 90 per cent of hate crime isn't merely invisible, it isn't actually a crime, as we would normally perceive it. It is a state of mind ... and not the sort of thing one can legislate against successfully ... it is searching for the invisible, the indefinable and the unprosecutable.'

Rod Liddle, *Spectator*

A ten-year-old boy was prosecuted for calling another boy a 'Paki' in the playground. There have been reports of five-year-olds being logged on a register or database, to monitor future homophobic or racist behaviour. There were suggestions that a dislike of spicy foods might be deemed significant in certain circumstances.

How large a problem is racism in schools?

Over five years, there were 95,000 racist incidents recorded in schools up to 2007.

Is this a lot or a little?

Over five years, and in 24,000 schools, that amounts to 0.8 incidents per school, per year.

In the name of the Merciful ...

In Australia, Pastor Daniel Scot was charged, tried and found guilty of incitement against Muslims in a lecture explaining why he had fled his home in Pakistan.

Ken Livingstone invited the preacher Sheik Yusuf Al-Qaradawi to London and dismissed critics as 'Islamophobes'.

Al-Qaradawi's views on

1 The death penalty for homosexuals:

Homosexuality is 'a reversal of the natural order, a corruption of man's sexuality, and a crime against the rights of females ... concerning the punishment for this abominable practice ... should both the active and passive participants be put to death? While such punishments may seem cruel, they have been suggested to maintain the purity of the Islamic society and to keep it clean of perverted elements.'

2 The use of children in suicide bombing:

'We cannot say that the [Israeli suicide bombing] casualties were innocent civilians. They are not civilians or innocent ... The Israelis might have nuclear bombs but we have the children bomb.'

56

3 On the destruction of the Jews:

'O God, destroy the usurper Jews, the vile Crusaders, and infidels. O God, destroy them along with their supporters.'

4 On dialogue with Jews:

'Iniquity on the part of the Jews is a great iniquity, grave iniquity, iniquity that is incomparable and overt ... we should not conduct a dialogue with these [Jews] while their hands are stained with our blood.'

5 On female genital mutilation:

'Anyone who thinks that [female] circumcision is the best way to protect his daughters should do it. I support this, particularly in the period in which we live.'

6 On the 2004 South Asian Tsunami:

'People must ask themselves why this earthquake occurred in this area and not in others. Whoever examines these areas discovers that they are tourism areas ... where the forbidden acts are widespread, as well as alcohol consumption and drug use and acts of abomination ... and sexual perversion ... Don't they deserve punishment from Allah? '

Extracts taken from *MEMRI* (www.memri.org)
and *Islam Online* (www.islamonline.net)

Dutch filmmaker Theo van Gogh's film made with Somali-born MP Ayaan Hirsi Ali campaigned against the abuse of women under Islam. After the film [*Submission*] was released he was murdered in the street by an Islamic fundamentalist.

'The film', according to one cultural relativist, Rohan Jayasekera was 'an abuse of his right to free speech'. Why? Van Gogh was a 'free-speech fundamentalist on a martyrdom operation' and 'he roared his Muslim critics into silence . . . effectively censoring their moderate views as well'.

He wrote: 'The inevitable violence of their response was grist to his mill,' and concluded by calling on us to 'applaud Theo van Gogh's death as the marvellous piece of theatre it was.'

(quoted extracts taken from Rohan Jayasekera, Associate Editor of *Index on Censorship*.)

Damien Hirst's art has used cows' heads to represent Christ's apostles. To represent the violent history of the Christian Church, these heads have knives, scissors and glass stabbed into them.

Various questions present themselves: Would this be legal under religious hate-crime legislation? If it used the heads to make the same point about Islam would it be legal? Would Damien Hirst have made the same point about Islam in Holland, after the murder of the filmmaker Theo van Gogh?

It is against the law to search more than two members of the same ethnic minority in any one domestic flight in the United States.

'If you denounce the views of Scientologists, Moonies, Satanists, Catholics or Islamic jihadists you may be liable for a seven-year prison sentence under the Anti-Terrorism and Crime and Security Act.

'We are now heading back to the world before the Reformation where robust debate about religion is illegal and offences produce exile or imprisonment.

'Why did the Government ever decide to introduce this law? Critics allege that it is pandering to the Muslim vote and trying to tap the religious Right. It was initiated by [the then Home Secretary] David Blunkett, whose speeches on the subject suggest that he may have been the victim of mistaken legal advice.

'He incorrectly claimed that the new law would "protect people and not ideologies" and that the exiting Public Order Act was inadequate to protect Muslims from serious harassment – which is not the case. False hopes seem to have been raised in Muslim communities that critics and apostates will be jailed for blaspheming against Islam.'

Geoffrey Robertson QC, *Evening Standard*

Almost £900,000 was spent by police over 22 months in order to steward illegal street meetings by the radical cleric Abu Hamza and others. After he was arrested on an extradition warrant other speakers continued delivering sermons (taster from one Abu Abdullah: Muslims 'must die for the sake of Allah and not live for the sake of unbelievers'). Public complaints that police were helping the groups to commit the offence of obstructing the highway were ignored.

'God created human beings pretty much in their present form and at one time within the last 10,000 years or so.'

This statement has been researched by Gallup in America in 1982, 1993, 1997, 1999 and 2001 on a base of 1,000 respondents. It has never drawn less than 44 per cent agreement from the American population.

~

'She [the Roman Catholic Church] holds that it were better for sun and moon to drop from heaven, for the earth to fall and for all the many millions who are upon it to die of starvation in extremest agony ... than that one soul ... should commit one single venial sin, should tell one wilful untruth ...'

In the light of religious-hate laws, will it be legal to republish Lytton Strachey's commentary on Cardinal Newman? Or Martin Luther's writings on the Pope?

The Theory of Evolution: The Great Myth

The US is 33rd out of 34 developed countries in the percentage of adults who agree that species, including humans, evolved.

~

'The question we must ask is: Is it more logical, rational, and scientific to believe in evolution, or is it more logical, rational, and scientific to believe that "In the beginning God created"? Let's look at the evidence.

'Does life arise spontaneously by chance, as evolution teaches? No! The basic axiom of all biology is biogenesis: Life only arises from life; it does not come from nonliving matter. Does this more logically fit evolution or creation?

'What about the teaching of evolution that everything is evolving ever upward to greater and greater complexity, all by chance? The evidence is the second law of thermodynamics. The laws of physics show that everything goes from organization to chaos. This is known as entropy. Does this more logically fit evolution or the biblical account of creation and the fall?

'What about the fossil record? Darwin said that if evolution were to be true we would find the evidence in the fossil records by finding millions of transitional forms or "missing links". What we find, in fact, is everything appearing fully formed after its own kind in the fossil record with no evidence of transitions! Does this more logically fit evolution or the biblical creation? In Genesis Chapter 1 doesn't God say He created everything, "after their own kind"?

'It never ceases to amaze us that when we were in kindergarten they taught us that a frog turning into a prince was a nursery fairy tale, but when we got to college they told us that a frog turning into a prince was science! The Bible says that only a fool says in his heart, "There is no God". By following evolution we have literally become a nation of fools following false, unscientific data.'

Ron Carlson, www.myfortress.org/evolution

A group called Christian Voice harassed a cancer charity in Scotland, Maggie's Centres, early in 2005 until it agreed to return a donation from the cast of *Jerry Springer – the Opera*.

~

'Of the 16 billion people who have been born since *Homo* became *sapiens*, I doubt if more than 500 million have lived in a world free of belief in magical causation or the threat of arbitrary imprisonment and death at the hands of religious police for thought-crimes. Afghanistan is a good place to ponder one's good fortune in being born in the modern West and not in a culture where malaria is treated by yelling, or the best cuts of meat are reserved for the dead, or it is believed that the motions of the stars are controlled from the liver of a rogue elephant, or divine honours paid to shallow depressions in the ground. We have the Enlightenment to thank for this, the moment when the West achieved intellectual maturity (or rediscovered that of the ancient world and reduced religion to a matter of opinion and turned the mullahs into comic turns like Rowan Williams. The Orientalist witch-smellers and post-modernists at Oxford have the Enlightenment in their sights. It is a sobering thought that whole cultures and educated elites can commit intellectual suicide.'

Matthew Leeming, author of *Afghanistan: A Companion and Guide*, about the response of Oxford intellectuals to the plight of women in Afghanistan

A solar-radiation-powered gravity-field generator

'According to the Cayce readings, the powerful Tuaoi Stone, or "Terrible Crystal," was designed by Atlanteans and used for a variety of purposes over thousands of years. Used positively, it provided communications, rejuvenating rays, and finally devolved to being used as an energy source for daily life in Atlantis. Its misuse on two occasions, however, caused 1) the sinking of parts of the Atlantean subcontinent near the Sargasso Sea and 2) the final demise of the Atlantean civilization itself.

'How was this device constructed? What was its source of energy? The Hutton Commentaries subscriber John Sutton researched these questions ... His concept of the design of a laser-powered crystal is based upon two recent papers from the peer-reviewed literature of physics.

'Currently, private industry is investing significant capital for the development of controlled nuclear fusion. Such an energy source would provide all of the world's energy needs from fuel extracted from sea-water. Atlanteans, possibly in a similar situation, may have undertaken research that resulted in the Tuaoi Stone. Energy beams from the Tuaoi (pronounced "too-oye") source were said to have powered vehicles that could travel both through the air and under water equally well. (Perhaps that is why no one has found any roads at the bottom of the Atlantic Ocean, where Atlantis is supposed to have been prior to 12,000 years ago.)'

The Hutton Commentaries (www.huttoncommentaries.com)

Education

Charles Cowling taught English for 25 years in state and independent schools. He generally got his classes to read the twelve books of *Paradise* Lost instead of the two on the syllabus. He retired to teach literacy in prisons. After he had done so for a year, it was found he had no teacher-training certificate and was required to take a Non-Vocational Qualification every week for two years.

An instructor came to sit in on his class, which consisted largely of murderers. They talked about the relative pronoun for an hour. Cowling was marked down to within a point of failing for 'not complying with his lesson plan'.

A former professor and head of the physics department at the University of New Mexico has, at the time of writing, been teaching at the grammar school in High Wycombe for the last three years. His subject is so popular that a third of the 450-strong sixth form are studying physics at A-level. The education authorities have told him his qualifications are inadequate – he must take his maths GCSE or leave the school.

The Teacher Training Agency said Professor David Wolfe could use the fast-track route to qualified-teacher status, which requires the submission of a portfolio of evidence. The Department of Education and Skills ultimately – and after a media outcry – allowed Dr Wolfe to continue to teach after submitting to a short teaching assessment.

~

The number of graduates rose by 70 per cent in the decade to 2007. The estimate of a graduate's extra earnings over a lifetime has fallen from £400,000 to £100,000.

Students face an average of £23,000 debt.

The proportion of graduates in nongraduate jobs has risen from 22 per cent in 1992 to 33 per cent now (figures apply to males).

~

'When I did my O-levels in 1986, we were asked to translate a 15-line chunk of a speech by Cicero to the Senate, in Catilinam, attacking his enemy who'd conspired against Rome in 63 BC. And we'd never seen the passage before – that's why the exercise was called an "Unseen". Ciceronian prose is nice, pellucid stuff, full of lovely rhetorical tricks. In one passage we had to translate, Cicero demonstrated the ancient art of the tricolon: arranging words or phrases in triplets, often of ascending lengths, for dramatic effect. "Your native land which is the mother of us all, hates you and dreads you and has long since decided that you have been planning nothing but her destruction. Will you not respect her authority, bow to her judgement, or fear her power?"

'Last year's GCSE passage concentrated on Cicero's speech about a conman called Pythius. Pythius fooled a Roman gentleman, Cannius, into buying a country estate with supposedly excellent fishing rights by paying some fisherman to fish in front of the grounds on the day Cannius inspected the property. The questions were fantastically simple: "Who was Cannius?" "What kind of work did Pythius do?" The only question that involves any translation says: "Pick out two Latin words which describe Cannius and translate them."'

Harry Mount, *Spectator*

〜

A distinction in the ABC cake decoration course is worth more points (55) than an A in an academic course such as maths, English or science.

〜

The Organisation for Economic Cooperation and Development says British state schools are so bad that the advantage of being privately educated here is greater than in any country except Uruguay or Brazil.

Eton came 195th in the official league table (this almost certainly says more about the league tables than about Eton).

~

One class at Intake High School Arts College in Leeds had 26 supply teachers in six months. The Alex Dolan secret-camera documentary for Channel 4 on the subject had a class left for an hour with the instructions, 'draw a picture of your favourite food'. A teacher normally working at a nearby school says in the film: 'I've been drafted in basically to give support to this department while HMI (Her Majesty's Inspectorate) are in. It's a bit of a con job, really.'

~

'I don't mind there being some medievalists around for ornamental purposes, but there is no reason for the state to pay for them.'

Charles Clarke as Education Secretary, contributing to the debate on the funding of universities, *Times Higher Education Supplement*

~

'The proportion of student debt to graduate salary is set to double in the next generation (42 per cent now, rising to 83 per cent in 2023).'

KAE: Marketing Intelligence, Futurology Report, for Liverpool Friendly Society

~

New league tables allow a D-grade pass in health and beauty, or leisure and tourism, or cookery, to gain a school 68 points compared with 58 points for an A* pass in maths, English and science.

Thus, a school at the bottom of the league tables could improve its position if it persuaded pupils to ditch maths and English and concentrate all their efforts on a GNVQ plus one other subject. Research published by the *Independent* revealed that many are doing just that.

One vocational qualification at GCSE is deemed to be the equivalent of four Cs in English, maths, physics and chemistry. So, a GNVQ in one subject and a pass in one other subject counts as five GCSE passes. Seventy-nine of the 100 'most improved schools' have benefited from this way of measuring academic achievement.

More than 600 students who have not achieved the minimum requirement to train as doctors (three grade Cs at A level) are being or will be paid for by the government. Universities, including Oxford, Cambridge and Imperial College, London, receive additional funding for accepting underqualified students.

Supporters of the whole-word-recognition technique of learning to read get very angry about phonics (that is, cuh ah tuh spells 'cat'). Barry Stierer, senior lecturer in the School of Education at the Open University, says that reading tests 'only provide a crude measure of children's ability to decipher decontextualised print, or to comprehend unseen text which is read for no real purpose'.

To 'decipher decontextualised print' is what lay people call 'being able to read'. It is one of half a dozen indicators of reading ability. A child might excel in five of the reading indicators without being able, in lay terms, to read.

'A recent report from the Basic Skills Unit showed that one in five adults are functionally illiterate.

'The national literacy strategy repeatedly uses the expression "to read on sight" – memorising how words look. This results in a high level of failure. The alternative, which is infinitely more successful, is to learn words by the sounds of the letters. Learning to read this way is called phonics (or synthetic phonics). It has two main elements, both of which are relatively straightforward. First, the child needs to be taught each of the letter sounds. The other element is to learn how to "blend" the sounds together to read words.

'A child who knows the letter sounds, and can blend, is able to read new words that he or she has never seen before. By contrast a child taught to "read on sight" will know only the words taught so far. Faced with new words – even a simple one such as "hat" – the child is likely to say that he or she has not done that one yet.

'At the end of a first year at school, children taught with phonics in the way I have described typically have a reading age 12 months ahead of those taught to memorise words by sight. More importantly the failure rate is far lower. Children whose teaching is based on sight vocabulary have a one in four chance of failing, with boys much more likely to fail than girls. With phonics less than one in 20 have this risk, and boys do as well as girls.

'All this is well known and has been confirmed by one published study after another. The best start for children is to learn all the letter sounds as soon as they start school. Commercial phonics schemes are available that ensure this happens in the first term, and they are widely used by teachers. Sadly the national literacy strategy recommends taking two and a half years to learn letter sounds.'

Chris Jolly, Jolly Learning Ltd, publishers of the Jolly
Phonics programme

'A seven-year study showed that pupils at schools that taught intensive phonics rather than the official method were on average three-and-a-half years ahead for their age in reading by the age of 11.

'Children from disadvantaged homes did as well as those from richer backgrounds and, far from falling behind girls, the boys were 11 months ahead at the age of 11.'

Professor Rhona Johnston of Hull University and Joyce
Eatson of St Andrews University – seven-year study of
Clackmannanshire schools

'At school, they had to recognise whole words in reading books and one day John came home upset saying he had been told off by his teacher for the stilted way he was reading. I had explained to the teacher that the boys would be de-coding rather than memorising words, but she continued to correct my son's method and sent messages to me in his reading diary. One read: "He is relying heavily on phonics to decipher new words. He would benefit from making sentences with the words in order to see the whole word in context." The boy felt caught in a crossfire and I gave up and let him do it the school's way.'

Liz Lightfoot, *Daily Telegraph*

Half of all boys leave primary school unable to read properly.

Ofsted Report, February 2005

'We just want to make the World a Better Place'

Alastair Campbell's diaries were very revealing. As diaries can be.

As a whole, the media ('media scum') leave much to be desired. They are 'mad', 'wretched' and 'poisonous'. The press are a 'bunch of shits'. The *Mail*: 'just basically right-wing shits'. '[Paul Dacre, *Mail* editor] and his paper are evil.' Also, 'the guy from the *Sun* was a total wanker.' In general, 'our disgusting right-wing press' is composed of the Lobby ('those fuckers'), sketch writers ('a sad little bunch'), photographers ('a pathetic bunch') and journalists such as those covering the Labour election launch from a school assembly full of hymn-singing children: a 'cynical bunch of wankers'.

Other named journalists include Simon Jenkins ('total wanker'), 'the little shit [Matthew] Parris', Jim White ('twat'), and John Simpson is one of a number of 'thin-skinned wankers' (later, Simpson is a 'precious arsehole').

Then there is 'that cunt Jonathan Oliver', with Adam Bolton 'still being a total cunt'. Stephen Glover comes out of it relatively well. He is merely 'a deeply unpleasant man'.

Black Rod is 'the little fucker' and Bernard Ingham is a 'silly old fucker'.

'I said I was sick of dealing with wankers.' Naturally. 'I hated these people.'

*

Alastair Campbell's successor as head of strategy and planning in Downing Street was Damien McBride. His downfall came when it was revealed he planned to publish a number of slurs, smears and rumours and put them out on a Labour propaganda site. They included the idea that the then Conservative leader, David Cameron, had contracted a sexually transmitted disease and the then Shadow Chancellor George Osborne posed for photographs at university in 'a bra, knickers and suspenders' and his face 'blacked up'.

*

The government backed off its commitment to introduce a Corporate-Manslaughter Bill. It had promised to introduce the Bill in response to the Paddington rail crash. But then it was pointed out that the legislation, which would allow company directors to be prosecuted, and perhaps imprisoned for negligence, could be used to prosecute ministers. The conundrum was solved by exempting government ministers.

Top Twenty legislative hits from the 2000s

1. All offences are arrestable.

2. There are 4.5 million DNA samples held on police files.

3. Damaging GM crops can be defined as 'a terrorist act'.

4. In 2001 two peace campaigners were prosecuted for causing 'harassment, alarm and distress' to US servicemen at their base in Britain by standing at the gate holding a placard reading 'George W. Bush? Oh dear.'

5. A minister can declare a state of emergency and suspend all legal proceedings, including Parliament.

6. The penalty for breaking an antisocial-behaviour order can be five years in prison.

7. Anyone's Internet history – the sites you have visited, who has emailed you and whom you have emailed – can be called up by public servants in a dozen departments, as well as all local councils.

8. A journalist's second email requesting information from a council press officer was designated 'harassment' and sent to the police.

9. The presumption of innocence is no longer an inviolable legal principal.

10. People wearing satirical T-shirts in a 'designated area' have been detained under the Prevention of Terrorism Act. The City of London is a permanently 'designated area'.

11. Police may take, and retain indefinitely, DNA samples (by force if necessary) from people who have been arrested but neither charged nor cautioned.

12. The existence of an interception warrant (to monitor Internet activity) is a state secret, and the penalty for revealing its existence to the person concerned is five years imprisonment.

13. It is a criminal offence to prevent an inspector from entering a nursery school for the purposes of inspection and punishable by a fine of up to £2,000.

14. Trial by jury may be abolished for certain cases.

15. Hearsay evidence is now permitted in court.

16. Double jeopardy has been abolished.

17. Bad character can now be produced as evidence of guilt.

18. Britons can be extradited to America without any evidence of wrongdoing being presented.

19. Under the Inquiries Act 2005, the powers of independent chairmen to control inquiries has been removed and given to government ministers.

20. Any cabinet minister may make 'emergency regulations' if he believes an emergency has occurred, is occurring, or will occur.

John Catt was wearing a T-shirt proclaiming 'Bush Blair Sharon to be tried for war crimes, torture, human rights abuse' and, lower down, 'the leaders of rogue states'.

The stop-and-search form filled out by the police officer stated, under grounds for intervention, 'carrying plackard

[sic] and T-shirt with anti-Blair info'. The purpose of the stop-and-search was stated as 'terrorism'.

～

The DNA database helps solve 3,666 crimes a year. That is, 0.3 per cent of 1.3 million crimes solved every year (with very nearly five million crimes a year being committed).

～

There is an International Obesity Task Force. Its chairman, Professor Philip James, says that 'the global obesity epidemic is out of control' and that this 'could halt economic progress in many developing countries'.

The Task Force turns out to be a private pressure group 75 per cent funded by drug companies who manufacture slimming aids.

The Social Issues Research Centre called the obesity claim a 'wildly inaccurate doomsday scenario', which used an out-of-date method of calculating obesity 'to support inappropriate health policies'.

～

Stealing a mobile phone now carries a maximum prison sentence of five years. A mobile costs £80 – about a working man's daily wage. You have to go back to the late eighteenth century, to a period famous for its judicial severity to find criminals suffering a five-year prison sentence stealing goods to the value of a working man's daily wage.'

Independent sketch

～

'As he [Bill Clinton] headed for his presidential limo, he stopped, shook me by the hand and said, "Thanks for everything." I said, sincerely, that it had been a pleasure and an honour to work with the greatest all-round communicator of the late twentieth century. He ... replied that it had been a pleasure working with the best communications adviser in the world.'

Alastair Campbell, in his Saturday sports column in
The Times

A study conducted by the Harvard School of Public Health in 2004 surveyed the health habits of 300,000 people – the most comprehensive study yet of its kind. The study found that the much-loved food pyramid popularised by the US Department of Agriculture actually contributes to rising levels of obesity. And, according to a study published by Duke University Medical Center, North Carolina, the bottom tier of the pyramid, including pasta, rice and bread (foods it says we're supposed to eat more of) causes the most excessive weight gain, whereas meats (second tier from the top) contribute much less to obesity.

The performers at Live8 – the charity concert to alleviate the world's suffering poor – were welcomed with 'goodie bags' worth $7,000.

Having argued in print for parents to have the choice between single jabs for measles, mumps and rubella (MMR) and the three-in-one cocktail, the newspaper columnist

Peter Hitchens received a letter attacking him. 'It was beautifully word-processed, perfectly spelt and very well researched. At the heart of it were these words: "I was one of those worrying parents, but it had nothing to do with being responsible. In fact, I was irresponsible because I ignored government advice and delayed vaccination which nearly cost the life of one of my children. I mistakenly thought mother knew best, and was fool enough to believe what you and your newspaper were feeding us." '

Peter Hitchens says that, when he eventually made contact with the woman, 'I was able to confirm the following things. She had never written to me. She has two grown up children in Africa. Neither of them has been ill through not having the MMR. She lives alone. She does not read the *Mail on Sunday* and could, therefore, never have seen any articles I had written about MMR . . .'

~

The average couple of whom one partner has a job is £1 a week better off than the average workless one-parent family. A lone-parent household with two children costs the public £11,000 a year in benefits.

~

Yvette Cooper, Shadow Secretary of State for Work and Pensions, told the House of Commons that a married couple with two children earning £25,000 a year paid no tax at all – or that all the tax they paid was given back to them in benefits.

~

'The Opposition is in a terrible fix. They can't win policy arguments, very often because the policy they are attacking used to be theirs. They say they'll cut waste, but the government says they'll cut even more waste. And then blame the Tories for being the party of cuts. And then, in an acrobatic innovation, turn their own job-cutting pro-gramme into a massive increase in public sector jobs. Thus, [the then Tory Shadow Chancellor] Oliver Letwin pointed out that the gross figure for 84,000 job reductions in the civil service turns into a net figure of a 250,000 increase.

'Mr [Paul] Boateng blandly replied: "The civil service is smaller today than it was in all but one year under the Conservatives."

'This contemptuous answer was technically correct and therefore more contemptible than any of the Prime Minister's claims about WMD. The Tories inherited about 750,000 civil servants and over the next 18 years reduced them by about half.'

Independent sketch

'He considered the outpouring of Tsunami compassion from the Treasury. Wasn't it the case, Mr [Vincent] Cable [of the Lib Dems] asked, that Indonesia's debts weren't actually being cancelled but merely postponed for a moment and that the postponed payments were being rolled up in the capital and would eventually attract interest? So far from enjoying debt relief, Indonesia would be paying "interest on the interest".'

Independent sketch

The 2005 league tables showed that the proportion of pupils achieving five good GCSEs fell. Three years later, more than a third of sixteen-year-olds left school without reaching the standard. The Prince's Trust estimated that half of all school leavers would leave school with a D or below in English or maths.

There may be as many as three million young people who have failed to achieve five good GCSEs since 1997.

Meanwhile, the number of A grades has risen to more than a fifth.

British social mobility – the chance of a child outperforming his or her parents – is the lowest among our major partners.

Just the job

Extra spending by 12 per cent produced improvement of public services of 4 per cent – the difference being made up of wage rises, administrative costs and such jobs as:

Health Development Co-ordinator for Healthy Eating, Haringey Primary Care Trust

You will develop, implement and manage the New Opportunities Fund "Five A Day Programme". The aim of the programme is to increase the consumption of and availability of fruit and vegetables to the communities of Edmonton and Tottenham.

The programme specifically targets:

* Schools in those areas of the boroughs with the highest health needs. This will involve encouraging schools to

adopt a whole school approach to healthy eating, providing training where necessary.

- Communities where the consumption of fruit and vegetables is low. The Co-ordinator will work closely with local communities: training community nutrition assistants, exploring the opportunities for Food Co-ops, Farmers Markets and Allotments.

Or ...

Strategic Energy and Sustainability Manager, Haringey Council

Reporting to the Head of Strategic Sourcing, your objective will be to ensure that sustainability is recognised as a key priority across the council. You will need to work closely with other departments developing the corporate framework and ensuring it is embedded in their business processes. You will be responsible for the procurement of the Council's energy supplies in accordance with Best Value and take forward the partnership working in relation to the agreed sustainability objectives.

Salary: £33,642 to £35,928

The BBC has advertised for a Head of Change 'responsible for shaping and managing the execution of the change ambition'. Interestingly, the organisation that hired a Head of Story Development was the Ministry of Defence.

The longest job title, according to the Plain English Campaign has been tipped from its place. 'Part-time health-care team foot health gain facilitator' has been edged out of first place by Lancashire County Council's 'temporary part-time libraries north-west inter-library loan business unit administration assistant'. When the post was advertised there were no applicants.

*

'Midge Ure was so appalled by the suffering he witnessed during his visit to Ethiopia in March 1985 that he vowed never to go back.'

Independent

*

'How Gordon Brown acquired a reputation for stability is a modern mystery. In the last seven years we've had a furious boom, house prices doubled, our international competitive position crashed, our stock market slumped since he taxed £5bn a year from its main investors. The savings ratio has halved. Pension funds are folding all over the country. And his much-vaunted job-cutting strategy in the public service includes hiring an extra 360,000 public servants. These outreach officers and passive smoking co-ordinators have pension rights that will be dragging this country backwards long after the Chancellor is wrapped up in his bath chair sucking at his last remaining tooth, and enjoying a parliamentary pension that is more, gentle reader, than your current salary.

'On Third World debt he was more than usually nauseating. He insists that Third World countries "open their books and become more transparent, to show where the money is being spent". This from the man who obfuscated Britain's accounts so thoroughly you couldn't tell how much we were spending on school buildings from one year to another. This from the man who invented statistical spin in his triple reannouncements of the same spending plans. This from the man who said: "90 per cent of our aid goes to the poorest countries in the world." Thanks to Rachel Sylvester we know that, on the contrary, management consultants alone soak up a fifth of the government's aid budget (trousering £3bn in the last five years). Were you aware that 20 per cent of your aid tax goes to KPMG?'

Independent sketch from 2005. Everything referred to became more obvious as time went by

∿

'Some of the girls were as bad as the boys. One female sociology student told me that her deaf cleaner (who also had a limp) should never have been employed because, being unable to hear the command "Not now!", she had regularly interrupted her work on "Class, Disability and Interpersonal Relations."'

Catherine Maskell, *Spectator*

∿

'Between 1950 and 1995, Western countries gave away around £1 trillion, in 1985 prices, in aid to poorer countries ... much of the money that has poured into poor countries since the 1950s has simply leaked back out – often to bank accounts in Switzerland. One recent study of 30 sub-Saharan countries calculated that total capital export for

1970–96 was some £187 billion, which, when accrued interest is added, implies that Africa's ruling elites had private overseas assets equivalent to 145 per cent of the public debts their countries owed. The authors of that study conclude that "roughly 80 cents on every dollar borrowed by African countries flowed back [to the West] as capital flight." '

Niall Ferguson, *Daily Telegraph*

At a figure of very nearly $4 billion a year, America spends more on aid to its cotton farmers than in aid to Africa.

'Mr Brown's talk of creating enterprise is certainly rubbish. If a university professor has an academic idea commercialised and receives in return a quarter share of a new million-pound company he will be immediately hit with a tax bill for £80,000, even before the company has turned over a cent or made a penny profit. If Gordon Brown thinks that encourages enterprise he's nuts. He probably does; he probably is.'

Independent sketch

International aid is given by poor people in rich countries to rich people in poor counties (Lord Bauer's grim definition). It may have been just coincidence that President Mobutu's wealth almost exactly matched the external debt of Zaire, but the source of the money is not in doubt. It is not the cruel banks that have robbed the Africans but the Africans' own leaders.

A scar on our conscience

'A Scottish backbencher opened up questions to the prime minister with a piece of wither-wringing information. She said 150,000 Africans die from malaria every month. She was quite valiant about it and the House went sharply into one of its moods, thrilling to the sentimental pleasure that pulsed through the benches.

'You have to agree, it does seem to be quite a lot of dead people. Every month, month after month. The numbers add up: it must be close to two million people a year. It's amazing we don't care about it more. I stand astonished at my own indifference. I expect you do too. The prime minister addresses the matter somewhat differently. He feels it to be a scar on his conscience. Or was it a scar on our conscience? Probably on ours, knowing the prime minister.

'Either way, we can assume that, broadly speaking, he is fractionally against this African holocaust rather than fractionally in favour of it. Therefore he is paying the interest on various inter-government loans for a month or so. This bold proposal always draws gruff approval from parliamentarians of all sides.

'It would be wrong, broadly speaking, to make a direct comparison between Tony Blair and Adolf Eichman. Neither Mr Blair nor Mr Brown has personally designed a malevolent solution to the practical problems of genocide. On the other hand, they're prepared to live with the Common Agricultural Policy, which impoverishes the third world and bans their exports and dumps subsidised food on them destroying their markets. They are also happy to spend billions on our own Regional Outreach Obesity Inspectorate Co-ordinators rather than kicking in an extra few billion to eliminate malaria.

'But Mr Blair does have a wonderful feel for what it is that people want, so it must be our fault in the end. He does what we want done.

'Time will tell. In a century or so, we voters may very well be thought as moral equivalents to provincial members of the Nazi party. We didn't actively want a holocaust, but we managed to avoid the sound of the trains (or in this case the television pictures), and we all found many perfectly good reasons to vote for leaders who said they were going to help but who didn't really do very much.

'NB: Some ass behind Mr Blair suggested we "send them some education". It would "make them self-sufficient". Maybe we could send them our examiners who could devise a marking system which showed they were already educated, without the cost of the schooling.'

Independent sketch

World-Class Public Services

'Hackney Parking Services are on a journey, one that recognises that a parking strategy driven by a commitment to the highest standards of customer care is the only effective way of delivering real benefits to the people, businesses and road users of Hackney. It's about backing respected parking enforcement strategies with a customer service ethos.'

Hackney Council website

The 2004 Omnibus Survey monitoring trust in official statistics:

'... the majority of respondents believed official figures were changed to support a particular argument (68 per cent), that there was political interference in their production (58 per cent) and that mistakes were suppressed (69 per cent).'

Also, the majority of respondents (59 per cent) 'did not agree that the government uses official figures honestly when talking about its policies'.

~

A nurse, Margaret Haywood, secretly filmed episodes of abuse of elderly patients. She was struck off, for breaching patient confidentiality. (She was reinstated in 2009.)

~

Public spending over the last decade has been slightly more than twice the trend of public spending in Britain since the war.

The spending has resulted in a large increase in public sector employees. The doctors, teachers and nurses we hear about, but also inspectors, quality-control officers and assessment officials reporting to and fro to check on whether the money is being spent effectively. The more public money that is disbursed, the greater the responsibility of the state to check on it.

As a result, the regulatory framework gets ever finer, the list of instructions sent out from Whitehall gets ever more detailed, the increase in unexamined, unscrutinised legislative effluent from Parliament becomes increasingly scandalous, because we can't muster the energy to witness it.

The marvellous thing about this is that no one is planning it, no one is responsible for it, and no one can stop it. It is a vast, collective, hive-like endeavour driven by its own incentives. We can only marvel at it.

~

Three photo captions in the Daily Mail *relating to Bristol Royal Infirmary:*

- Filthy stains cover the floor beside a seating area in the Old Building.

- Open to view: The inside of a cleaner's cupboard with rubbish on a trolley.

- Cockroach beside the drink carton that was left there for three days.

～

The Staffordshire Health Trust Chief Executive resigned after the publication of a report into his organisation. The report, by Robert Francis QC, contained the following observations:

'There were repeated accounts of poor continence and bladder care, particularly in respect of frail and elderly patients ... patients being left on commodes for far too long, requests for assistance ignored and patients left in sheets soiled with urine and faeces ... reports of staff being dismissive of the needs of patients and families struggling to fill the gaps in poor nursing care themselves ...

'Meals placed out of reach or were taken away before they could be touched. Visitors had to assist other patients, yet were sometimes prevented by staff from helping with feeding ... Incontinent patients were left in degrading conditions and some patients were left inadequately dressed in full view of passers-by ...

'Rooms vacated by patients with *Clostridium difficile* were not always cleaned before the next patient was admitted.

Witnesses described how they had to undertake cleaning themselves ... patients and their families were often afraid to raise or repeat requests for help or concerns for fear of upsetting staff and causing a reduction in care. Such diffidence was not hugely surprising in the light of the attitudes of some staff to patients when they needed help. I heard of a nurse telling a patient not to "moan", of another who appeared angry when asked for toileting help and of yet another who mocked a patient's religion ...

'The staff evidence persuaded me that a culture of bullying and fear was prevalent in the Trust among staff. I heard of a fear of bullying being a possible explanation for more staff not coming forward with concerns. There was at times a forceful style of management, which was perceived as being bullying even if it was not intended to be so ... a lack of trust in management to the extent that there appeared to be a widespread disbelief in the assurances given that there would be no adverse consequences for approaching the inquiry.'

The Chief Executive presiding over this was given a £400,000 payoff and a £1 million pension pot.

Directly after the government announced the job cull of more than 104,000 civil servants, they advertised nearly 1,000 public service jobs with salaries worth £36 million, including:

- Liveability manager, Havant Council – £45,000

- Integrated Enforcement Co-ordinator, Office of Deputy Prime Minister – £33,000

- Improving Working Lives Co-ordinator for North London Strategic Health Authority – £29,000.

- And ... Female Learning Mentor, Co-ordinator of Structures and Arrangements Framework, Customer Accessibility and Inclusion Manager, Project Officer for Historic Landscape Characterisation, Senior Outdoor Access Officer, Welfare Rights Manager, Senior Disability Equality Officer, Peripatetic Welfare Benefits Caseworker, Parenting Skills Co-ordinator.

NB: The then Chancellor's announcement of 104,000 civil service job losses should be viewed in the context of an extra 860,000 extra civil servants since coming to power (with the attendant pension rights of around £700 billion).

Royal Mail employees who turn up to work for six months will be eligible for one of 34 cars or one of 68 holiday vouchers worth £2,000.

Strange case of the dog that barked ...

Alison heard her Twickenham neighbour's burglar alarm go off while they were on holiday, so she rang the police. Two policemen turned up and stood outside the house listening to a dog barking.

'Are you going to go in?' Alison asked.

'We can't go in if there's a dog in there,' one said.

'That dog barking isn't in there, that's our dog. It's in our house next door.'

'We can't go in if we think there's a dog in there,' the other said.

'But what are you going to do. The alarm's ringing. There may be a burglar inside right now.'

'Tell you what,' the first officer said to Alison, 'We'll go round the back and if they come out the front, you stop them.'

~

A constituent of MP Tony Wright woke up in hospital after a massive heart attack. To get onto a waiting list he was put down for a cardiac assessment and sent home. Patients are not deemed to be waiting for treatment until assessed. A year later he was still waiting for assessment. 'As a result of the increased investment, all waiting times are down in the NHS,' Tony Blair often said.

~

Number of reorganisations the NHS has undergone in 20 years: 19.

~

UK train fares lead Europe's. The first £1,000 train fare was announced in 2009, a first-class walk-up ticket from Newquay in Cornwall to Kyle of Lochalsh, in the Scottish Highlands.

Private cataract operation

EU average cost: £600

UK average cost: £1,500

Our eye surgeons do ten private cataract operations
and charge a fee of £800 a time (an income
approaching half a million a year for one morning a
week).

'Twenty-six million people of working age have levels of
literacy and numeracy below those expected of school
leavers.

'People with the lowest levels of skills – those expected of
a 9- to 11-year-old or below – can experience practical
difficulties in their everyday lives.'

National Audit Office report

Some London postmen have demanded extra money to
work until two in the afternoon. This has, in fact, long been
the official end of their working day, but they have become
so used to bunking off early that now they see it as a right
to be compensated for actually working the hours for which
they are paid.

The government's £50 million journey planner recommends the best way to travel between any two points.
The trip between the Lancashire resorts of Fleetwood and

Blackpool should be a 45-minute bus ride. The website recommended a two-and-a-half-hour journey consisting of three walks, two train trips and a bus ride.

John Thurso, the Liberal Democrat's then transport spokesman tried the system and found the recommended journey from Scotland to Westminster would take 16 hours and 26 minutes compared with the seven hours it usually takes him. It also tells motorists they can travel the 12 miles from east to west London during the morning rush hour in 53 minutes.

～

'She was admitted to casualty and I was anxious that she should not have to wait on a trolley for a long time. I was pleasantly surprised, therefore, when she was admitted to a ward within a few hours. I was told that she would be operated on the next day. Anyone with any medical knowledge will know that it is important to operate on a fractured neck of femur within a maximum of 48 hours, whatever the person's state of health or age. As is the normal custom, my relative was designated nil by mouth, but she went on being nil by mouth for five days, until eventually I threatened to go to the press unless she was operated on.'

Angela Browning MP, House of Commons

～

Hospital patients with little hope of recovery should be allowed to die of starvation or dehydration because it costs too much to keep them alive, suggest government papers which set out the views of then Health Secretary John Reid.

They should be denied the right to food or water if they fall into a coma or become too ill to speak for themselves.

Victims of, for instance, cerebellar ataxia, a degenerative brain condition that affects 2,500 Britons, would be starved to death on the NHS as they lay conscious but powerless to protest.

~

'When socialism has socialised health, you have (that is, everyone has) a duty not to be fat, not to smoke, not to contract sexual diseases. Your selfish behaviour takes up scarce resources. Others pay for your treatment so they have a right to tell you how to go about your life. Actually, it's their duty. Very soon the government will be (what's the most ridiculous thing you can think of?) ... demanding the right to give teenage girls compulsory contraceptive injections? What, they are already? There you are, then.'

Independent sketch

~

A heart bypass in the UK costs £12,000. In India, £2,000.

~

James Campbell, 69, had a successful double knee replacement in Ahmedabad, western India. This would have cost him £20,000 in England, but he got the surgery, flights and a seven-week stay for £8,000. Another Scot, 55-year-old Alex Cooperwhite, flew to Goa for surgery to heal a back complaint the NHS said was incurable. He paid just

£1,500 for surgery, intensive care and physiotherapy – and his 'incurable' problem was cured immediately.

It's very hard to say how many needless deaths the former government is responsible for because it doesn't keep proper figures. It doesn't count them accurately, it says it's too difficult. There'd be an outcry if the true body count were known. Some people put it at 5,000 over a year, some say 20,000. Others say it could be double that because the people who are responsible for the killings are the same people responsible for reporting them. The incentives are misaligned, you think? It's hard not to agree.

These deaths aren't confined to the smoking cities of Iraq and Afghanistan, incidentally, as we continue to 'stabilise' them. No, these are the deaths in the NHS caused by a standard of hygiene that predates the Crimea War. The modernisation programme seems to have stalled. This must be galling for a government that was aspiring to moral totalitarianism and ethical omnipotence. For all its bullying and all its billions this was a government that couldn't make nurses wash their hands.

Tony Blair, then Prime Minister, rose to the occasion. The best form of defence is the smear. 'Let us remember who forced the contracting out of cleaning!' he cried. There's nothing wrong with contracting out in principle, but it does require people who can write contracts. 'We pay you money, and in return' – secret ingredient follows – 'you clean the hospital.'

Councillor Paul Clokie, the leader of Ashford Borough Council, has suggested that local people sponsor the mending of potholes in their roads. In Louisville, Kentucky, the fast-food chain KFC fixes holes and puts its logo on the new surface.

✐

'Because Alan Johnson has only been in his Work and Pensions job four weeks he gave us access to an awesome fact (he won't be doing that again). He told the House that the department spent £5 billion in the last seven years on "modernisation". That's cash out. Nearly 10 per cent of the savings gap spent on – oh, who knows what.'

Independent sketch

Healthy debate . . .

In a debate on hospital-acquired infections, which are directly responsible for 5,000 deaths a year and may be indirectly responsible for a further 15,000:

'[It] is nothing less than an outrage that the infection control teams reported to the NAO [National Audit Office] that 12 per cent of them had requested bed or ward closures but had been refused [in order to meet targets for waiting times]. The situation is worse than that. I asked a trust chief executive if he had refused such a request. He said:

'"They know our situation so they won't ask."

'Only a few days ago, a consultant told me of an exchange in an internal hospital meeting when the infection control consultant said that MRSA [the killer bacterium methicillin-resistant *Staphylococcus aureus*] ... persisted because the trust had overridden advice to shut wards due to the need to achieve waiting-list targets. The chief executive had agreed to that.'

Andrew Lansley, Tory then Shadow Health Secretary, *Hansard*

'The Secretary of State for Health (Dr John Reid): I beg to move, To leave out from "House" to the end of the Question, and to add instead thereof: "welcomes the Government's commitment to ensure that patients can have confidence that National Health Service hospitals are clean, safe environments with infection firmly under control; congratulates the Government on its action plans for reducing infection rates, 'Winning Ways' and 'Towards cleaner hospitals and lower rates of infection ...'"'

Hansard, same debate

For all the dozens, hundreds, thousands of targets, directives, instructions, summaries of best practice and in spite of the new tertiary qualifications required of NHS staff – it is still impossible to get nurses to wash their hands.

'One of the worst PFI [Private Finance Initiative] deals we have seen.' The Public Accounts Committee's verdict on the Libra project to computerise magistrates' courts. Eleven thousand computers from Office World cost you less than £5 million. For the government they cost £390 million over eight years.

'I rang a mother to tell her that her son had told me to "f*** off", and she seemed flabbergasted that I was informing her of something so trivial.'

> Teacher on *The Times Educational Supplement*'s online
> forum about unruly pupils

'The delay had nothing to do with staffing or pressure of patient numbers – both were average for a Saturday night ... However, just out of our sight there was a traffic jam of trolleys – more than 20 of them, bearing patients waiting in corridors and cubicles for beds, tying up space and staff who might otherwise have been available for us.

'The beds were unavailable because patients who were well enough to leave hospital but needed nursing care had nowhere to go. And why did they have nowhere to go? Because the Government has imposed such expensive fire, health and safety regulations on nursing homes that large numbers of them in the area have had to close. With no alternative accommodation, patients are having to stay in hospital instead, blocking beds to those who really need them ...

'So here we have a state-of-the-art hospital – typical of many, I suspect – unable to look after its casualties because red tape has ensured that the community has no provision for those who have been treated and cured.'

> Magnus Linklater, *The Times*

If you believe this is really what Britain is like you'd commit suicide. This isn't to say any of the following is untrue, unfairly reported or distorted. Maybe it is, maybe it isn't. But the papers are full of it:

Her Majesty's Government suppressed a report proving ill-equipped, barely trained teenage soldiers are being mutilated in Afghanistan while at the same time Tony Blair, the First Secretary and the Foreign Office conspired with an Islamic regime to release a mass-murdering terrorist in order to get cheaper oil from Libya. This has enraged the US and negates the only reason we are in Afghanistan: to keep our 'special relationship' with them.

Meanwhile, General Sir Richard Dannatt, who has spoken out against the action in Afghanistan, has had his expenses published – possibly in a smear attempt by the Defence Ministry. Generals have had their first-class train travel revoked.

Council chiefs on salaries higher than the Prime Minister's go on free trips to Cannes while hiking council tax, restricting rubbish collection, prohibiting cake sales at fairs on health-and-safety grounds and insisting traditional gatherings be policed by marshals. NHS bosses fiddle the figures to show government targets are being met while patients die.

Banks make one-way bets whereby they collect enormous bonuses if they win and taxpayer bail-outs if they lose. They don't understand – because nobody can – what the odds are in their bet.

Unelected quangos, authorities and public servants are engaged in an unofficial revolution to monitor, restrain, intimidate and control the British people, to suppress their instincts and reprogramme their behaviour. They can retire ten years before private-sector workers, and on lifelong index-linked pensions.

A dog was attacked by thugs; they attempted to set it on fire. The same thing happened to a five-year-old girl battling cancer.

The government is paying a generation of morbidly obese teenage mothers to breed an underclass whose largest contribution to society is to stimulate the narcotics trade and appear on reality TV shows. Their mothers are on prescription antidepressants. Their children kill each other and innocent bystanders with knives.

Academic results rise every year while performance falls as free-market exam boards make their papers more accessible to flatter schools and please politicians. Classroom behaviour makes learning impossible, which is why a quarter of all school leavers are illiterate.

Meanwhile, on the lighter side of the news, a murdered Playboy model was so badly mutilated she could be identified only by her breast implants.

Maybe it's us. That is, the print media. Maybe every portrait is a self-portrait and we in books and newspapers fear we are going to be doomed, ruined and mutilated by the Internet, and this picture of Britain is a product of that paranoia.

Or is that wilfully optimistic?

It All Depends How You Look at It

Proportion of British men feeling entitled to regular sex with their partner:	66 per cent
Proportion of British women feeling the same:	47 per cent

Delayed discharges from hospital have plummeted. However, this category is calculated on the basis of acute beds blocked. The authorities have deemed many 'acute beds' to be 'intermediate beds' and intermediate beds aren't counted in the figures for delayed discharges.

Research published in the *Health Service Journal* has shown a number of techniques for falsifying NHS statistics.

There is a target stating that 90 per cent of patients should wait less than four hours in A&E. In order to meet this target, the health trusts notified the hospitals when the inspection would take place. The hospital managers cancelled leave, put doctors on overtime and drafted in agency nurses. Routine operations were also cancelled to ensure there were free beds so that patients could be quickly transferred from A&E.

Witney A&E closed in the evening to allow its staff to be diverted to help the John Radcliffe A&E in the test period. When asked if this wouldn't interfere with Witney's ability to meet the target, David Cameron, the local MP, was told: 'If the ward isn't open there isn't a target to meet.'

Other techniques included renaming corridors as wards, taking the wheels off trolleys to turn them into beds, deeming reclining chairs to be beds, and driving patients around in ambulances outside the hospital (the four-hour wait began to be registered only when patients were deposited in the A&E ward itself).

Despite hitting an average of 92.7 per cent of patients waiting under four hours during that week, rates dropped immediately. One Northwest hospital that met the target is now running at a 65 per cent average. An A&E consultant at the hospital said: 'The way the targets have been met is totally fraudulent.' He described how on one day in April, his department fell as far as 52 per cent.

Taken from the *Health Service Journal*

A survey of 200 hospitals by the British Medical Association revealed that eight out of ten accident and emergency units admit they discharge patients too soon, give them substandard care, or send them to the wrong wards in order to meet the government target for four-hour waits.

The government said at the time that 96.8 per cent of patients are seen within four hours.

'This gives a deliberately distorted picture of the changes that have taken place ...' John Hutton, for the government, said (of the BMA survey).

~

Same date, same story, two reports ...

Guardian: 'Higher rates are cooling house-price growth. The Halifax said the monthly increases in property inflation levels had eased during the last 12 months.'

The Times: 'House prices rose at their fastest annual rate in more than a year according to figures from Halifax released yesterday.'

~

'Every survey of public opinion indicates overwhelming support for [ID cards]. In Erdington and Kingstanding, I would estimate that four out of every ten people are in favour of ID cards.'

Sion Simon MP

> In 1983, proportion of
> A-levels marked A: 7 per cent
>
> In 2003, proportion of
> A-levels marked A: 22 per cent
>
> In 2008, proportion of
> A-levels marked A: 26 per cent
>
> 'Don't let anyone tell you that standards have
> dropped because more of you have done well – this
> is simply a myth.'
>
> David Miliband, then Schools Minister, to
> A-level students

A report by the Qualifications and Curriculum Authority showed that a fall in the pass mark was a key reason for the increase in the numbers of children passing the National Test in English between 1996 and 2000. The report found that the pass mark of the reading element of the test should have been five marks higher in 2000 for the test to have been of the same difficulty as in 1996.

Independent research by the Curriculum Management and Evaluation (CEM) Centre at the University of Durham found that, while the proportion of children passing the English test increased between 1996 and 2000, the actual reading and writing abilities of children had not changed.

Jeffrey Robinson, senior examiner for the examination board OCR, revealed that the pass mark for the harder paper of GCSE maths had fallen from 48 per cent in 1989 to 18 per cent in 2001.

The CEM Centre showed that the standards of A-level maths fell by a full grade between 1996 and 1999. It also showed that the standards of subjects such as physics were significantly harder than subjects such as business studies.

The Engineering Council reported that internal tests set by university departments had found 'strong evidence of a steady decline over the past decade of fluency in basic mathematical skills and of the level of mathematical preparation of students accepted onto degree courses'.

In 1989, the mark required to achieve grade C in the higher Oxford and Cambridge GCSE mathematics paper was 48 per cent. In recent times it has been as low as 18 per cent. So candidates could get four out of five questions wrong and still achieve a top grade.

Figures from the government exams watchdog, the Qualifications and Curriculum Authority, showed that students were given A to C grades for progressively lower marks in maths and English over a five-year period from 1997.

The marks needed to gain an A grade in the higher-tier section of the Assessment and Qualifications Alliance's maths GCSE dropped by eight percentage points from 65 per cent in 1997 to 57 per cent in 2002.

The mark required for a C on the same higher-tier paper fell from 30 per cent to 21 per cent over the same period. Mike Cresswell, Director General of the Assessment and Qualifications Alliance, told *The Times Educational Supplement:* 'Boundaries have to be able to move if we are going to maintain standards. '

'Negri recently described the Soviet Union as "a society criss-crossed with extremely strong instances of creativity and freedom", which is more than he has ever said about a democracy. He even says that the Soviet Union fell because it was too successful. I point this out and he replies: "Now you are talking about memory. Who controls memory? Faced with the weight of memory one must be unreasonable! Reason amounts to eternal Cartesianism. The most beautiful thing is to think "against", to think "new". Memory prevents revolt, rejection, invention, revolution."'

Johan Hari of the *Independent* reports on his encounter with old communist Antonio Negri

*

'It is beginning to be racist for teachers or social workers to object to autocratic patriarchy and submission of women within many Muslim communities.'

Polly Toynbee, *Guardian*

*

Women are forbidden to drive or swim in Saudi Arabia; they need the written permission of a husband or male guardian to leave the country, move home or be admitted to hospital.

*

The British Crime Survey excludes murder, crimes against children under 16, sexual offences, dealing in and taking drugs, and shoplifting (total of such crimes estimated at around 12 million a year).

Recorded crime shows an increase of 850,000 in the last five years. Gun crime doubled, robbery up 50 per cent, violent crime up 83 per cent.

'Crime is down by a third overall,' governments say.

*

'... [F]urther leaks suggest even more serious fiddling of the system at ministerial level. According to several sources in the immigration service and an internal memo, the Home Office condoned a policy of not pursuing illegal immigrants who were already working in Britain for fear that, if caught, they would simply claim asylum. David Blunkett, the [then] Home Secretary, has staked his reputation on reducing the number of asylum claims.

'It is true, as Blunkett points out, that most migrants are genuine and skilled workers. But it is now clear that thousands of people, including possible terrorists, have been allowed to enter and stay in Britain without proper checks.'

David Leppard, *Sunday Times*

*

The number of adults in this country without a job has remained more or less constant over the last two decades; but as unemployment has fallen, so disability has risen.

There are now two and a half times the number of people who are supposedly too ill to work as there are who are simply unemployed, and this at a time when the population is getting healthier.

*

How many people work for the government? Or, more precisely, how many people depend on the government for their income?

At the end of 2009 there were:

- 6 million public sector workers
- 5.8 million on welfare
- 12.5 million on state pensions

Total: 25 million

Private sector workers: 22 million

The state owns the hospitals, the schools, several of the banks and most of the workforce, and is spending 52 per cent of GDP. Are we there yet?

～

Road maintenance costs £2.7 billion a year. It will no longer be counted as public spending but deemed to be 'investment'. When he was Chancellor, Gordon Brown decreed that borrowing would not be permitted for 'spending' but only for 'investment'. It may be why, shortly after New Labour came to power, he began calling all public spending 'investment'.

～

One of Gordon Brown's first actions as Chancellor was to reorganise the Red Book (the book of government accounts) by changing many of the headings. This made it impossible to compare the current year's spending on any one item with that of the year before's.

～

From Richard J Evans' **In Defence of History:**

'The academic Paul de Man was discovered to have written numerous articles for a Nazi newspaper in Brussels between 1940 and 1942. After his emigration to the USA, de Man never mentioned this to any of his colleagues or pupils, and indeed always denied any kind of collaborationist involvement in Belgium during the war ... [He] became an extremely influential literary theorist, leading the "Yale school" of literary deconstructionists who argued for the irrelevance of authorial intentions and the multiple indeed virtually infinite possibilities of textual interpretation ... Literary criticism, for de Man seemed to be a way of denying his own past.

> 'It is always possible to face up to any experience (to excuse any guilt) because the experience always exists simultaneously as fictional discourse and as empirical event, and it is never possible to decide which of the two possibilities is the right one. The indecision makes it possible to excuse the bleakest of crimes because, as a fiction, it escapes from the constraints of guilt and innocence.

'[The French-Algerian philosopher Jacques] Derrida suggested that only deconstructionists were properly equipped to understand de Man's writings, and called his critics "confused, hurried, and rancorous professor-journalists" whose work was a heap of muck destined for the intellectual compost heap, and whose views were "dishonest", "obscene", "venomous", "uneducated", "indecent", "grotesque", and "laughable".

'Like much postmodernist writing, the defence of de Man by the deconstructionists was riddled with contradictions. On the one hand, Derrida and his supporters insisted theoretically on the infinite possibilities of textual interpretation; on the other they argued in practice that to interpret de Man's early writings as collaborationist or anti-semitic was just plain wrong.

'On the one hand, the author himself had no control over the meaning of what he wrote; on the other, Derrida denounced in the most polemical terms those he thought were wilfully misunderstanding what he said in de Man's defence. On the one hand, everything, including anti-semiticism, was a text, and all texts were theoretically subject to the infinite play of significations; on the other, Derrida denounced anti-semiticism as "essentially vulgar".

'On the one hand it was wrong to prioritise elite culture over popular culture, one kind of text over another; on the other, de Man's defenders bitterly resented the involvement of journalists in the debate, and clearly loathed its escape from the elitist discourse of academia . . .'

Richard J Evans

Why do neo-Nazis deny the Holocaust? Haven't they quite got the hang of Nazism?

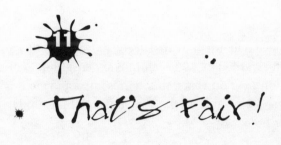

That's Fair!

In 2004 the directors of Network Rail were given bonuses of £400,000 to share, even though punctuality had declined.

In 2009, a year after the enormous bail-out, City banking bonuses reached £6 billion (down from the £10 billion paid in 2007).

In 2009, the head of Northern Rock was paid £1.3 million. The taxpayer-owned bank lost £383 million in the same period.

During the boom, the three government regulatory agencies that were supposed to be reining in US banks gave out $19 million in bonuses.

The average pay for a chief executive of a Standard and Poor's top 500 company was nearly $11,000,000 in 2008.

Men in America have median earnings of $45,000

*

It was estimated to have cost £14 million to dismiss Sven Göran-Eriksson, the England football manager.

*

Jewish slave labourers who survived Nazi death camps have been awarded £4,500 each in compensation. Reduced for inflation over 50 years, this represents a payment of £1 a week for 72 hours' work. That is something under 1.5 pence per hour.

*

'I began to raise criticisms of Opus Dei with my director but he told me these were really criticisms of myself.'

John Roche, former Opus Dei member

*

A lorry driver who was convicted of careless driving after killing a family of four was fined £1,000 by Luton Crown Court.

A former primary school head was jailed for three months for tampering with and adding answers to Key Stage 2 SATs papers.

Michael O'Leary, a TV aerial installer, was jailed for manslaughter for four years for strangling his wife to avoid giving her half the £440,000 he had won six years earlier.

The young idiot who pretended to be a police officer and walked into a royal party at Windsor castle pleaded guilty to a charge of 'public nuisance' – he was given four-and-a-half years.

Shell revealed it had been overstating its oil reserves by over a fifth. It paid fines of £65 million to the US Securities and Exchange Commission and £17 million to Britain's Financial Services Authority. The company's exploration and production director resigned. He was given a £2.5 million pay-off.

Sixty-seven-year-old Mary Hudson from Staffordshire has had bricks thrown through her window, incendiary devices left outside her house, a life-size rag doll with a noose round its neck and a knife in its chest left at her front door. Three vehicles owned by her children have been sprayed with acid (resprays costing £3,000). Her daughter received a note saying, 'If your mother doesn't quit within one week we can't be responsible for what happens to you – so can you please display these yellow cards in the bedroom where your children sleep?' She received a threat that the body of her husband, who recently died of cancer, would be dug up. Mrs Hudson is the cleaner at a farm where guinea pigs are bred for research purposes, and the Animal Liberation Front claimed responsibility.

Petra Ecclestone (Bernie's wife): 'I buy all my eggs from my people in Croatia. I take the plane over and buy them from the peasants ... my girls don't like English eggs.'

Agriculture subsidies in the
developed world: £1 billion a day

America exports rice to Haiti, and the EU exports
tomatoes to Ghana.

Oxfam report: Trade barriers cost the developing world
twice what they receive in subsidies (£100 billion a
year).

Insurance companies and credit reference agencies are not
bound by the terms of the Data Protection Act. And any
commercial organisation is allowed to use for any purposes
the data you provide during your transaction provided it
gives the opportunity to refuse (the box to tick). The box
doesn't work if the owners depersonalise the information –
the organisation can then use your postcode to sell to junk
mailers.

A credit card charging up to 70 per cent interest is marketed
under the slogan 'Stay in control of your budgeting'. It is
aimed at individuals (whose credit histories are all
available through credit rating agencies) who have been
rejected by other lenders – often because they have run into
debt problems in the past.

To export €1 worth of sugar costs €3.30 in subsidies.

Oxfam says that the 49 very poor sugar-producing
countries are allowed to sell the equivalent of the sugar

grown on 15 farms in Norfolk while being priced out of their home market by EU sugar dumped below the market price.

~

'Conrado, a qualified nurse [was] brought from Asia to Britain by an agency to work in a hospital. He and others had to pay £700 to agencies, followed by a months deposit and rent for accommodation. When they started in the NHS, their monthly pay of £805 was cut to £198 or £46 a week, after deductions were made at source by the NHS trust and handed to the agency.'

The same report – from the International Labour Organisation – also cites cases of Indian nurses in private care homes under contract to the state being charged £3,000 for registration.

This part of the ILO (International Labour Organisation) report was suppressed by the Department of Work and Pensions – who paid £20,000 towards the research costs – until after the British elections in May.

~

A virus can get into your home through your dial-up phone line, install itself secretly on your computer and wait until you've gone to bed. Then it dials up a premium number (often a sex line) and keeps the line open for hours (or possibly for days or weeks if you are on holiday). British Telecom insists you pay the phone bill even though you have been the victim of a trespass and a fraud and even though they have collaborated in it and profited from it.

~

'What difference is there between foxes and fish? None in law, only the difference which ministers won't admit: that Labour backbenchers would fight as fiercely to protect the working-class killing of fish as they fought to ban the upper-middle-class killing of foxes. The symmetry is underlined by the two tests that Number Ten wanted to apply to hunting: that it could be licensed only if it served a useful purpose and was carried out in a way to cause least suffering.

'Angling is a pastime, not a necessity. As for cruelty, the practice of livebaiting, in which anglers impale fish on double or treble hooks through their lips and body in order to catch predatory fish, letting them struggle in agony until they are eaten by another fish or left to die of their injuries, is at least as nasty as what happens to foxes.'

Christopher Hudson, *Independent*

A judge dismissed socialite Patricia Duff's claim of $1.6 million a year from Revlon billionaire Ron Perelman. She wanted $135,000 a month in child support. The judge said that child support is not designed to fulfil the mother's wish list – otherwise it simply becomes 'adult support'.

'Where I worked, cleaners lost 15 minutes' pay if they were more than five minutes late. Many had housing problems but could not afford the time off to deal with them. They were allowed 30 minutes off for lunch, unpaid. In our working area there were no seats, so staff who spent all day on their feet took their 15-minute break crouched on their haunches or perched on plastic dustbins. When they washed the dishes, the cleaning company rationed the amount of detergent used ...

'Over the past 20 years the number of NHS cleaners has fallen by some 40,000, during which time MRSA cases have soared.'

Carol Midgely, *The Times*

Middle-class enrolment at university has risen to 50 per cent. Enrolments from non-professional backgrounds have risen at half the rate to 18 per cent.

The Sutton Trust commissioned research from the London School of Economics in 2004. It showed class divisions worse than in the 1960s. The housing charity Shelter says the division between owners and tenants was creating social divisions as deep as those in Victorian Britain.

We Want to Re-engage Ordinary People in Politics

'I don't want to live in a police state, or a Big Brother society or put any of our essential freedoms in jeopardy. But because our idea of liberty is not keeping pace with change in reality, those freedoms are in jeopardy.'

Tony Blair

(I think this means: 'To preserve our liberties we must abandon them.')

'At the Labour conference highlight, one David Hide sat down during Tony Blair's standing ovation. He held a placard saying "I'm sitting down for peace in Iraq". He was arrested. Perhaps that's too technical a term. He was taken by police from his silent, sedentary protest to the interview room, where he was told the Labour party had asked for his pass to be revoked. There was no explanation.

Five hours later he was told it had been an "administrative error".'

Independent sketch

～

The then Speaker Michael Martin put in place a £150,000 legal bid to stop details of MPs' expenses being made public. He argued the information was a 'substantial unlawful intrusion' into MPs' lives.

～

The government and the judiciary can continue to conceal the names of more than 170 judges who have been disciplined. The reason the tribunal gave? The judges would suffer 'great distress' if details of their misdemeanours were made public.

～

The 'secret memos' showing Tony Blair was committed to regime change in Iraq (against all UK legal advice), and that the evidence for weapons of mass destruction 'was being fixed around the policy', are still classified documents. Therefore they cannot be used in the Chilcot Inquiry. Yet text of the documents is freely available on the Internet, and indeed they have their own *Wikipedia* entry (search on 'Downing Street memo').

～

MPs were not allowed to see papers relating to the Anti-Counterfeiting Trade Agreement while they debated the Bill in Parliament in early 2010.

～

One month into the former government's 'new era of openness' the *Independent* publishes responses to its requests for official information:

Q: Please disclose the legal advice given by the Attorney General on the legality of the war with Iraq.

A: *No. It is exempt as legally privileged information (Attorney General).*

Q: Please disclose all ministerial and senior military officer correspondence on the subject of the legality of the conflict with Iraq.

A: *No. There is no obligation under the Act to disclose this information (Ministry of Defence).*

Q: Please disclose all the open evidence against the Belmarsh detainees.

A: *No, this would be too costly. Some of the information might also be exempt (Home Office).*

Q: Please disclose material concerning Stephen Byers' decision to declare Railtrack insolvent in autumn 2001.

A: *It will not be possible to respond to this request within the appropriate cost limit (Department of Transport).*

Q: Please provide minutes of meetings held between officials at the Department of Culture, Media and Sport and executives of US gaming companies.

A: *We need extra time to determine if this is in the public interest (DCMS).*

Q: Please let us see papers relating to the DTI investigation into BAT.

A: *The department holds such information but the information itself is being withheld as it falls under the exemption in section 44 of the Act (DTI).*

~

The way they talk makes it impossible for outsiders to understand what they are saying:

Peter Hain, then Minister for Europe, was asked in select committee: 'Do you think the early warning mechanism will make any difference in practice, given that the Commission could simply override the national parliament's objections?'

He said: 'It is a fair point, and we need to make clear what is new intrusion and what is an endeavour – including under the Regulation of Investigatory Powers Act 2000, for which my right hon. Friend the Foreign Secretary was responsible – to codify and pull in those things taking place around us. If we can do that – I respect those who believe that we were on the wrong trajectory, although, in fact, we were trying to do something that was totally misinterpreted and that looked, to the world outside, as if we were going the other way – we might get it right. I do not have a fundamental principled disagreement with that, as Parliament's role is to pull in, and to make sure that others do not have the right that the security and intelligence services have – under the kind of surveillance and review that they have – to intrude in other people's information or their lives. Getting that right will be important in future.'

Uncorrected proof of Select Committee
record of proceedings

~

Some wretched minister, now retired, issues a stream of meaningless verbal effluent to her select committee:

'The spending review is relevant not just in terms of how it will be allocating money over the next three years, but in some of the ways that we are looking at how we spend money and how we actually organise money, in a sense.' *(A spending review is a review of spending.)*

'For example, this year in the spending review we have spending groups which are interdepartmental and which are looking, for example, at spending in deprived areas and how we make that more effective.' *(We are reviewing spending in deprived areas.)*

'None of us expects that we will get all of that right within three years. We need to therefore be setting the programme now as to how we change spending in order to meet our overall priorities.' *(We want to spend money on the things we want to spend money on, so we are reviewing spending.)*

'That is a major theme of the spending review this year and that is why, in looking at the Urban White Paper, we have specifically wanted to do that in line with those considerations. They are not simply considerations for the next three years: they are considerations that will really move much further forward. If we are able to move them forward, that will enable the work that we want to do in terms of urban renaissance to be, I believe, much more fruitful.' *(A spending review will help spending.)*

Mr Cummings: Perhaps my second question is now superfluous. I was going to ask which rules you are proposing to abolish.

Hilary Armstrong: We are constantly looking at that. The better regulation task force from the Cabinet Office continually gets on to us about what rules we can get rid of and we are, with local government through the central, local partnership with local government, looking at what we can get rid of, but we have to be sensitive on that.

Chairman: Could you give us one example?

Hilary Armstrong: Off the top of my head, no.

Uncorrected proof of Select Committee
record of proceedings

∿

Radio advertisement to promote the government policy on university top up fees to young people:

'The mega news is that the darty government posse will help you through uni by shelling out the clam. You cough up zip till you are minted. So peg it, don't veg.'

And in another version:

'Here's stoking news. We're not bawling. The readies are waiting. Get on your grid and get busking. The darty government posse will help you through uni and you cough up zip till you're blinging.'

∿

John Prescott's department published its response to an analysis of the new Eurocode for building standards. It may have been dictated by the Deputy Prime Minister himself, as he was then.

'[It] is a country's right not to recognise an Informative Annex as being acceptable in that country; in such a case, the relevant National Annex must state that the Informative Annex is not accepted. If the contents of the rejected Informative Annex are covered in a suitable National document, a reference to such a document is permitted in the National Annex under the item "non-contradictory complementary information".

'From a Eurocode user's point of view, it will be somewhat inconvenient to jump back and forth from the body of the document to the National Annex. Unfortunately, an NSB is not permitted to publish a National version of the Code with the parameters from the National Annex incorporated into the EN text. Users of the Code may, of course, mark up their own copies of the Code with the values of the NDPs etc.

'The Eurocode recognises that alternative application rules, from those given in the Code, may be used, but they should not be contradictory. However, it is not permitted for National alternatives to be included in the BS-EN publication, either in the text or the National Annex. Indeed, guidance paper L and En 190 contain a warning that, if an alternative application rule is substituted for one in the Code, the resulting design cannot be claimed to be in accordance with the Eurocode, even if it meets the principle [sic] rules given in the Code.'

This was in reply to an analysis from the
Institute of Structural Engineers

Our Glorious Leaders

In the past few years:

Priests across the United States and Europe systematically abused children with beatings and sodomy.

Lawmakers in the United Kingdom looted the public purse with fraudulent and questionable claims on their expenses. This was ultimately exposed by the *Daily Telegraph*. Voters were none too pleased with their elected representatives.

When he was Prime Minister, Tony Blair took us to war in Iraq based on a number of whopping lies. These concerned weapons of mass destruction that it turned out Saddam Hussein did not have. One of his sources was the so-called 'dodgy dossier'.

Executives of large companies voted to up each other's salary and determine each other's bonuses. Government-owned banks continued to pay astonishing bonuses to their directors. Equitable Life reneged on the annuities it guaranteed; its members fought the case to the House of Lords and lost; Parliament has been unable to do anything.

Immigration, it was revealed by an official, was let rip in the early 2000s in order to 'rub the noses of the right in diversity'. There was a simpler reason: new, low-wage immigrants need public services and state support. They vote Labour.

~

The boss at Maidstone and Tunbridge Wells Hospital Trust, where 2,700 patients died of a superbug, sued to double her £75,000 pay-off. Rose Gibb had quit her £150,000-a-year job as chief executive in October 2007 after reports linked *Clostridium difficile* to deaths at three hospitals. She was originally offered a pay-off of £250,000, but the Health Secretary intervened and brought it down to £70,000. Then Ms Gibb sued to try to get it up to £150,000. The case was still ongoing in March 2010.

~

'[T]he Great Recession was caused by the smartest guys in the room saying, trust us, we understand how credit default swaps work, and they're great. No wonder so many Americans have decided that experts are idiots.'

Sharon Begley, *Newsweek*

~

The cost of bailing out UK banks has been estimated at £1.5 trillion.

Bank bonuses in 2007   £10.2 billion.

Bank bonuses in 2008   £4 billion.

Bank bonuses in 2009, as the age
of austerity began to bite   £6 billion.

~

Three MPs charged with fraudulent expenses claims – that
is, of stealing £60,000 between them – applied for legal aid
to defend themselves. While means testing for legal aid is
being introduced (those having more than £283 a week
have to contribute to their costs) the new system wasn't due
to reach the court dealing with them until after their trial.
'It's all within the rules.'

The police enquiry resulting in the three charges cost
£508,000.

The cost of prosecution could amount to £3 million.

~

The king of Swaziland fended off criticism of his personal
rule by international aid organisations with promises of a
written constitution. In the meantime his fabulously poor
country provided him with a half-million-pound limousine
with a 26-speaker stereo system. When the constitution was
produced, it may not have been quite what the World Bank
and International Monetary Fund were expecting: the most
important clause in it conferred absolute power and
perpetual authority to the king.

~

'But if mistakes were made, Lord Butler explained, they
were collective ones. Everyone was responsible so nobody
was to blame. Hang on, you want to say, if everyone was
responsible why doesn't everyone resign? You haven't got

the hang of this, I fear. If you've got a systemic, collective failure no-one is to blame unless they work for the BBC.

'But (you want to press this to the point of rudeness) if there was collective responsibility, shouldn't the person at the top answer for it? Well, so the Prime Minister did. He told the House: "I take full personal responsibility." It was one of those sentences that stopped before it finished. The complete sentence would have gone: "I take full personal responsibility so shut up."'

Independent sketch

∿

'We would have to reflect long and hard if we are to be the messenger who is continually shot.'

Gerry Adams, President of Sinn Féin, 9 February 2000

Pretty straight kinds of guys . . .

Tony Blair:

'I hope that people know me well enough and realise I would never do anything to harm the country or anything improper. I never have. I think most people who have dealt with me think I'm a pretty straight kind of guy.'

A little list of Labour sleaze allegations

In the New Labour years we saw the following:

Bernie Ecclestone donated £1 million to Labour and got an exemption from the advertising ban on tobacco for his Formula One racing business.

The Trade and Industry Minister had to resign over a £373,000 private loan from Geoffrey Robinson, the then Paymaster General, whom the DTI was supposed to be investigating over the Transtec affair. The minister (Peter Mandelson) resigned again following accusations relating to the passport application for one of the Hinduja brothers (although he was later cleared by an independent inquiry).

Geoffrey Robinson, accused of receiving £200,000 from Robert Maxwell, was more or less let off by the Standards Committee after being unable to locate the payment in his overseas trusts (the invoice had been published by Tom Bower).

Government advertising doubled between 1997 and 2001.

When the World Trade Center was attacked, special adviser Jo Moore sent out an email saying, 'It is now a good day to get out anything we want to bury. Councillors' expenses?' When she repeated the ploy at the funeral of Princess Margaret she was exposed by civil servant Martin Sixsmith (he was fired).

David Blunkett failed to declare the £700 a month rent he got from his home after he moved into the ministerial lodgings provided by the taxpayer.

Derry Irvine, the Lord Chancellor, asked for party donations from lawyers whom he had the power to promote.

Ron Davies resigned from the cabinet after being robbed by a man he'd met on Clapham Common and later resigned from the Welsh Assembly following accusations of gay sex (he claimed to have been badger watching).

Paul Drayson gave £50,000 to the Labour Party and later received a £17 million contract to supply vaccines to the NHS. He was made a peer in 2004, after which he gave the Labour Party a further £500,000 donation.

While the party was in financial difficulties it borrowed millions to fund its 2005 election campaign from people who subsequently became peers. The Treasurer of the party said he had no knowledge of the loans, which were subsequently investigated by the police. The Treasurer was Jack Dromey, the husband of Harriet Harman.

Six Birmingham councillors were convicted of a Labour vote-rigging fraud that would 'disgrace a banana republic'.

The Prime Minister's chief fundraiser, Lord Levy, was arrested by the police in the cash-for-honours investigation.

The Prime Minister's wife used a convicted fraudster to help buy two flats in Bristol.

A Sheffield MP was suspended for helping his assistant (a former male escort) in a bogus immigration application.

The Home Secretary claimed a rail pass for his mistress.

The Deputy Prime Minister was reported as having sex with his personal assistant behind the open door of his office (the words 'cocktail sausage' were included in the personal assistant's report).

A former energy minister resigned after an hour-long passage of sexual intercourse on the sofa in his office. He described the accusations as 'absolutely groundless' until the photographs were published.

Labour peers were stung in a *Sunday Times* operation offering to amend legislation for cash (£120,000 in one case).

The Home Secretary's husband claimed taxpayer's money for watching a soft-porn pay-per-view. She also said her sister's spare bedroom was her 'main home', allowing her to claim many thousands of pounds from the taxpayer (there were numerous other examples).

Gordon Brown's director of communications was fired after an email plot to slander Tory MPs with sex slurs.

Three Labour MPs were charged with theft – for claiming payments on mortgages that did not exist. Labour peers and MPs were acquitted by their own party-dominated committees because there was 'no evidence' they had planned to use the money for their own purposes. And then, of course, the expenses scandals – but they're a book all to themselves.

~

'Under New Labour only the future is certain. The past keeps changing.'

Paul Flynn, Welsh MP

~

Diane Inch, a 40-year-old Liberal Democrat councillor, was the inspiration and foremost member of the Healthy Eating Scrutiny task group. She was to be promoting healthy eating and the benefit of exercise to the Cheshire Borough of Halton. She was 19 stone, clinically obese and took no exercise. 'I may not be the perfect size ten but that does not mean I am unhealthy,' she said.

Halton council issued a statement saying: 'Members of the Healthy Eating Scrutiny group are chosen purely on merit and we are disappointed at the suggestion that personal issues such as this are considered to be relevant.'

～

From one of the former Prime Minister's African trips, healing the scar on the world's conscience:

Headline:

BLAIR'S JET IN 1,000 MILE ROUND TRIP TO PICK UP PRAWN COCKTAILS

～

'I've met more mad people in the Palace of Westminster than in all my years doing mental health social work.'

David Hinchcliffe, chair of the Health Select Committee

～

A round-up of President Niyazov's dictatorial eccentricities. He is the ruler for life of gas- and oil-rich Turkmenistan. Torture, disappearances, arbitrary detention, house demolitions, forced labour and exile are all features of life in Turkmenistan, and the president is the same sort of ally of the West in the War Against Terror as Saddam Hussein was in the 1980s in the war against ayatollah-based fundamentalism.

The offence of criticising the president (minimum prison sentence of five years) is known as 'parricide' and is defined in the criminal code as 'questioning the policy of the president'. Banned are: gold teeth, long hair, listening to the radio in the car, ballet. He named January after himself and April after his mother (who wasn't called April). He has decreed adolescence ends at 25 and old age begins at 85. He declared a national holiday in honour of the melon. He is building a $6.5 billion lake in the desert and has begun work on an ice palace in the foothills of the Kopet-Dag mountains, where summer temperatures reach 50 degrees Celsius. Children study for a maximum of nine years. Part of this will be in winter sports in the ice palace.

The pathology of the modern political class is the same all over the world ...

In Virginia, Algie Howell (67) got a Bill through the lower legislature banning thongs appearing over the tops of trousers. The Bill attracted international coverage when it passed through the lower house, and was killed by a unanimous vote in the senate. Mr Howell has also considered a Bill to stop people slouching while driving their cars.

Corporate killing: 'The Government considers that while there may be difficulties in proving a "management failure" there is a need to restore pubic confidence that companies responsible for loss of life can be held accountable at law.'

Government ministers are specifically excluded, making it impossible to sue the Minister of Health for the 240,000 preventable deaths in the NHS from defective hygiene since 1997.

'Just fuck off with your fucking stupid questions!'

Jack Straw, Foreign Secretary, to Owen Bennet Jones during
the recording of an interview on the World Service. Before
the interview was over, the producer had phoned the
Foreign Office to say that the words had been removed from
the interview and the tape wiped

~

'"Unstable states, like North Korea," political leaders keep
saying. But North Korea – whatever its many inadequacies –
is so stable that the head of state is Kim Il-Sung (Great
Leader) who died in 1994. His son (Dear Leader) carries on
in the shadow of his father, who wasn't just president-for-
life but president-for-ever.'

Independent sketch

~

'Travel by rail (which would have cost £97) was considered
but rejected as an option (by Prince Andrew's office), based
on the additional hour-and-a-half travelling time that
would have been involved and the potential unreliability of
the train arrival time.

'The Queen's helicopter was the preferred mode of travel
at an expected cost of £1,014 (£917 more than the £97 it
would have cost to travel by train). When the helicopter
became unavailable, a chartered helicopter was used at a
cost of £2,939, tripling the original cost and costing more
than £2,842 more than the option of travelling by train.

'We found no documentary evidence that the Household
reconsidered whether saving the Duke an hour-and-a-
half's travelling time, and doubt about train reliability

justified the extra costs involved in using a chartered helicopter.'

National Audit Office report

~

More hot air ...

In September 2004 Tony Blair said that action to reduce carbon emissions was essential to 'avoid disaster'.

A leaked text showed that senior government officials tried to remove a commitment from a European Union agreement to reduce carbon emissions. It was denied.

January 2005

Headline:

CARBON EMISSIONS LIMIT INCREASED

February 2005

~

The tongue is forked three ways ...

'I remember a few years ago, when at the BBC, interviewing the leaders of the three competing groups in the hunting debate, those for and against the ban and the "middle way" compromise caucus. Each had just been to Downing Street. Each told me Blair had told them he was on their side.'

John Kampfner, Observer

~

Iraq's President Iyad Allawi attracted unfavourable commentary weeks before the January 2005 elections when he concluded a press conference by giving journalists $100 cash each. Weeks before the British elections in May 2005, then Chancellor Gordon Brown sent £250 to all British citizens with children born in the last three years.

~

The Libyan media don't run down their leaders like we do ...

On the 30th anniversary of the Libyan revolution, a newspaper said of Colonel Gaddafi: 'His teeth are naturally immune to stain so that when he releases a full-blown smile they discharge a radiation pregnant with sweet joy and real happiness for those lucky ones around him.'

~

'No government would have allowed or legislated the Internet into existence if they had been able to see what it would do.'

William Gibson, Cyberpunk author

Parliamentary evasions

'I don't recognise the hon. Member's figures.'

'This must be seen in the wider context of the overall success.'

'I would have hoped the hon. Member would join in celebrating the achievements rather than offer carping criticism.'

'Well, that was a nice little rant.'

'No decision has been made.'

'We have no plans to ...'

'I am sure that Opposition Members would be the first to complain if they judged that Ministers at a distance in Whitehall were interfering with day-to-day decisions about military capability, which were made, quite properly, by those responsible on the ground.'

'This is always kept under constant review.'

'The important thing is ...' before going off on a long, therapeutic monologue, the only purpose of which is self-justification.

'The real question is ...'

'What the issue actually is ...'

'It is the subject of an investigation, and it would be inappropriate to comment in detail or to speculate on what the findings of the investigation might be.'

~

Tony Blair's brilliant consensual evasions always started with, 'I don't disagree with the central thrust of what you are saying at all ... I totally sympathise with the problem you're talking about ... I think that's a very reasonable way of putting the point to me ... From your question and the questions others have put, I suggest there isn't an essential conflict at all ...'

Labour's Bob Waring wondered how the Prime Minister squared Saddam's corpses and killing fields and mass graves with the fact that, up to the 11th hour, the evil old maniac was being offered a deal to stay in power. Ah, but the war was never about mass graves, the PM then says, it was about the UN resolutions. It wasn't about regime change, it was about changing the regime, a very different thing.

The then Tory MP Howard Flight asked an important question. Would the Prime Minister guarantee not to raise the upper level for National Insurance contributions? (There was a black hole they had to fill, after all.) The Prime Minister said, 'We have absolutely no plans to do so.'

What was he trying to say? It depends what the meaning of the words 'absolutely', 'no', 'plans', 'we', 'have' and 'to do so' is.

$\sim$

'David Miliband [sometime Schools Minister], the morning star, bears many important similarities to Tony Blair. Only some are to his credit. Let's not bother with those ones. Fresh-faced, sincere, honest, open as the sky, these are the qualities he deploys in the most ingenious ways. [Tory MP] Andrew Selous asked about the so-called "surplus places" rule. This rule stipulates that schools may not expand while other schools in the area have spare capacity. A good school that everyone wants to send their children to can't expand if there's a lousy school next door with empty places (because no one wants to send their children there). It's why only four schools, [then Tory MP] Tim Collins said, have been allowed to expand to the demand. Only under a state monopoly does such an onerous, impoverishing, life-denying, quasi-criminal racket work.

'Mr Selous claimed that some 70,000 parents had bought a house in a more favourable catchment area. He asked therefore whether this surplus places rule could be abolished.

'David Miliband beamed his fresh and open-faced smile at us and triumphantly declared that no such rule existed. "There is no surplus places rule!"

'This is true. Although there is a committee (which he chaired) that issues guidelines (not rules) that schools should not expand while there are places available in the same area.

'In a decade, Mr Miliband may be telling the House about his passionate belief that weapons of mass destruction held by some piffling dictatorship constitute a real, current treat to British national security and that we must invade them. We must remember, at that remove, what we heard in the House of Commons when he said the accurate and absolutely misleading thing: "There *is* no surplus places rule!"'

Independent sketch

Timing is everything . . .

Gordon Brown used the Exchange Rate Mechanism as a constant example of economic mismanagement by the Tories. He was himself robustly in favour of joining the ERM at the rate we went in at:

'I wish at the outset to welcome the Chancellor to his new position and I shall begin by saying what he should have said this afternoon ... He should have announced that he would open negotiations to join the Exchange Rate Mechanism.'

Gordon Brown, Hansard, 31 October 1989, col. 261

'Let me tell the Secretary of State what he should have said ... he should have told us that he has proposed to the Prime Minister that the Government should open negotiations to join the Exchange Rate Mechanism.'

Gordon Brown, Hansard, 22 November 1989, col. 127

'It is a [trade] deficit that reinforces the need for Labour's approach: an industrial policy to invest in training, research and development; a policy in the regions to ensure exchange rate stability, by opening negotiations to join the Exchange Rate Mechanism.'

Gordon Brown, Hansard, 6 March 1990, col. 736

'That policy [support for investment and manufacturing], combined with our commitment to the Exchange Rate Mechanism, seems to me a sufficiently substantial anti-inflationary policy.'

Gordon Brown, Hansard, 26 February 1992, col. 1049

'[T]here are those like Lady Thatcher who believe that Britain should devalue and turn its back on Europe and the Exchange Rate Mechanism with all the harsh consequences that would ensue.'

Gordon Brown, Sunday Express, 6 September 1992 – ten days before Black Wednesday

'Had Labour won the 1992 election, the first major event of Gordon Brown's Chancellorship would have been the

Exchange Rate Mechanism debacle. Then, 15 per cent interest rates and boom-and-bust would have been put on his account, the credibility of the Labour party would have been shattered for a generation and Gordon would have ended up up behind the 7-11 babbling endogenous-growth theory to a row of slumped rubbish bags.'

Independent sketch

∿

Britain *forward* not back – New Labour election slogan

The phrase occurs in *The Simpsons*, in which Clinton says during a presidential debate: 'My fellow Americans. We must move forward not backward, upward not forward, and always twirling, twirling, twirling towards freedom.'

Life is too complicated for sound bites...
Excellent! we'll put that on the campaign poster

We're just Trying to Make Things Better

Managers told the GCHQ board it would cost £20 million. It cost £400 million. The professional fees for the Treasury's new building (at £25 million) came to one-fifth of the total construction cost.

Figures from Richard Bacon MP,
member of the Public Accounts Committee

~

Civil service note regarding the purpose of the Millennium Dome. It 'is to re-energise the Nation.

'The ultimate aim of the Company therefore is to change perceptions, more specifically:

- to raise the self-esteem of the individual
- to engender a sense of pride in the wider community
- to enhance the world's view of the Nation ...'

~

Central government administration costs have gone from
£15 billion to £21 billion. In the Department of Work and
Pensions, fraud and error account for between £3 billion
and £7 billion. Customs and Excise lose between £7 billion and £10 billion on unpaid VAT on alcohol, tobacco
and fuel. Each year, £100 million is spent training teachers
who never teach. One failed computer system – the
Benefits Payment Card – cost £1.1 billion. The probation
service IT project had seven managers in seven years, five
of whom knew nothing about project management. The
project went 70 per cent over budget. The IT project for
the courts nearly trebled its original budget with the final
bill coming in at £400 million. The Government Communications Headquarters expected to pay £40 million for
moving the signals intelligence computer systems into a
new building.

The government-endowed e-university was given a budget
of £50 million and attracted 900 students.

If an £800,000 estate is divided equally among three
children and no steps are taken to avoid Inheritance Tax,
the government will take a larger share of the estate
(£214,800) than each of the children (£195,000).

Steve Dawe, spokesman for the Green Party in East Kent,
on the proposed wind farm for Romney Marsh, consisting
of 26 turbines each as high as a 30-storey building: 'We

are also optimistic about the wind farm as a tourist attraction.'

~

Regulations introduced between 2001 and 2003: 12,450.

Regulatory reform orders introduced by the Department of Trade and Industry in same period: 1.

~

Of Gordon Brown on British pensions:

'He took all the big decisions on pensions. He has wrecked the system of private pensions; he has wrecked the system of public pensions; he has destroyed the system of savings; he has taxed pensions, not openly but by deliberate stealth; he has impoverished generations of old people, past present and to come. Brown's pension policy has been one of the great disasters of British financial history.'

William Rees-Mogg, *The Times*

~

'Recently I travelled to the other end of the country to give a talk to doctors. They told me that a distinguished local consultant had been suspended for two years by the management, which was tired of her constant reference to deficiencies in the hospital. The management wrote to her patients actually inviting complaints against her. Not a single complainant could be found; quite the contrary, she was praised by them all. The management trawled her notes for errors, pouncing joyously on something they later had to withdraw when she was able to prove that she had been in the right.

'It is not difficult to see what the denouement of this story will be: her reinstatement at a cost possibly of several hundreds of thousands of pounds to the service. But her enthusiasm for her work will have been destroyed for ever, and the patients deprived of her good offices for a very long time. The managers who were responsible for this waste of life, talent, enthusiasm and money will be promoted.'

Theodore Dalrymple, *Spectator*

~

There is a plan proposed by California's South Coast Air Quality Management District to require all public vehicles to be powered by electricity, natural gas or other clean-burning fuels. However, this will use more hydrocarbon fuels, not less. Electricity is produced primarily by burning hydrocarbons and the energy delivered to an electric car requires more hydrocarbon fuel per mile than does the direct use of hydrocarbon fuel.

~

Drug companies reveal research showing 50 per cent of their medicines don't work. Placebos are as effective as medicines in one-third of cases.

~

'The process of strategic planning is like a ritual rain dance. The main objective is not to make it rain, but to become better dancers.'

Professor James Brian Quinn

~

'From the new year, Justin Bairamian ... will manage a team of audience insight managers that will work with production divisions to help programme makers use audience insight as part of a new programme development.

'His team will also work with audience research and commissioning teams to help bring audiences to the forefront of people's minds.'

From the BBC's online house journal

~

'Sir, I wrote recently to the managing director of my train company to complain about the reduction in the rush-hour train service to and from my local station.

'I received an acknowledgement saying that the managing director likes to reply personally. When the letter arrived the jaunty salutation "Dear McIntosh" seemed to start things on the right foot. It went on:

'By cascading our train fleet in such a way, enabled us to release more Turbo units to us, which subsequently allowed us to increase the stock formation of many of our Turbo's where previous capacity had been a major issue. Although I appreciate your dissatisfaction with your particular journeys, capacity has increased overall. We are still confident that the timetable is robust and whilst it may appear improvident to your journeys – the timetable must be seen as part of the whole and not in isolation.

'I have a vague sense that my complaint has been acknowledged as technically correct but judged, by virtue of its focus on my own circumstances, as morally unsound. It's hard to be sure.'

Neil McIntosh, letter in *The Times*

~

The Member of Parliament on the committee asks: 'Do we increase capacity or manage existing capacity better?'

The Civil Service, in the form of a 28-year-old social exclusion expert with a severe haircut answers the committee member: 'Both. But let me say this first. Centralised models of outreach can easily lead to inadequately targeting the money where it is most needed, which leads to the first question of how we can take people up the learning curve, as we move from preparatory stage to implementation both by reskilling and carrying out a comprehensive review evaluating the existing successes so far.

'So the forthcoming White Paper will draw together the broad range of current thinking. The draft National Strategy draws together the work of eighteen Policy Action Teams and a cross-cutting review of the government intervention in deprived areas forms part of the current spending review process. None of the Action Zones have actually surrendered their autonomy to a centre, they are a confederation in the way they operate. Everybody is committed in principle to the notion of partnership, and there is a partnership charter.

'But from our inspection and joint review activity we do not find a lot of correlation often between the level of resources and the quality of services. To revisit the objectives and decide whether they're still valid, we commissioned an independent survey, which confirmed in a more detailed way that we would like to expand that area of work using the regulation which says we have to provide information that helps policy makers assess the results of policies.

'National service framework, setting out the style of services to be developed with clear national standards, include the monitoring and reporting framework which will obviously build up and be synergised with sectoral indicator developments and with the environmental indicator developments and that is an important development for trying to put the whole monitoring and the reporting system into the policy context balancing short-term deliverables against long-term sustainable change and the reform of the legislative framework. The signs are in the right direction but there is a long way to go. To name and shame on a level playing field those straying from an acceptable benchmark.

'We see this as a ten-year programme.

'I am happy to expand on that further, if you would like me to.'

~

Les Watling, of the Darling Marine Center at the University of Maine, calculates that mobile fishing gear covers an area equal to all the continents' shelves (nearly 11 million square miles) every two to four years. He also estimates that nearly 6 million square miles of estuaries, bays, and continental shelves worldwide are bottom-scraped each year.

~

The last we heard, the EU was subsidising every cow to the tune of $2.40, when there are two billion people in the world who live – or exist – on less than $2 a day. Britain spends approximately £4 billion on the Common Agricultural Policy.

~

Hilary Benn: The World Bank estimates that up to half the gains from eliminating barriers to merchandise trade would accrue to developing countries, which could lift more than 300 million people out of poverty by 2015.

〜

Asian high-seas fishing vessels set drift nets up to 64 km (40 miles) long.

〜

The health centre in Ethiopia's Mekane Salam serves a community of 180,000 people but has no doctor.

Hansard

〜

VIOLENT VIDEO GAME SELLS OUT AFTER
BEING BLAMED FOR MURDER

'It's flying off the shelves for all the wrong reasons,' an HMV spokesperson said.

〜

'For a relatively long time it will be absolutely necessary that we quietly nurse our sense of vengeance. We must conceal our abilities and bide our time.'

General Mi Zhenyu, vice-commandant of the
Academy of Military Sciences, quoted by
Richard Bernstein and Ross Munro, authors of
The Coming Conflict with China, New Statesman

〜

It would take a Haitian worker 16.8 years to earn what the head of Disney makes in an hour ... The sales price of just one T-shirt in the US that the Haitians had themselves made amounted to nearly five hours of their wages.

The Administrative Terror

'We look increasingly to the state to know what to do, to be told how to behave. Should this police officer jump into a lake to pull out a drowning child? Or that citizen hit a rapist over the head with a brick. Should this young man take a course in website design? Or climb a ladder to fix the gutter? The state has the answer.'

Independent sketch

Nick Clegg – the man who became Deputy Prime Minister in May 2010 – put three, legally unrelated issues to the then Prime Minister, Gordon Brown. Five thousand schools are taking the fingerprints of schoolchildren as a matter of course; there are one million DNA records of innocent people held by the police; 1,000 requests a day are made for surveillance. 'The Prime Minister seems to see no limits,' Clegg said. 'He is creating a surveillance state.'

If only. The Prime Minister isn't creating it and has no power to stop it. What we have emerging in Britain is a general cultural movement in favour of surveillance. There is a growing sense that society generally and the state in particular should take an active interest in all individual activity. And that this is right, proper and inevitable.

~

The total net overrun on 240 key government projects was, by 2009, more than £19 billion (up 4 per cent from 2007).

In the Nimrod project the government were planning to get 21 fighters for £95m each. The cost per fighter turns out now to be £400 million.

The IT project for the NHS Spine – a set of national services used by the NHS Care Record Service – is currently 450 per cent over budget.

~

More serious data breaches have taken place within the NHS than any other UK organisation, according to the Information Commissioner's Office.

A total of 2,897 breaches were reported, accounting for more than 30 per cent of the total number, deputy commissioner David Smith told the Infosec security conference.

The NHS, which is currently introducing digital patient records, said that 113 incidents occurred due to stolen data or hardware, with a further 82 cases of lost data or hardware.

information from the *Health Service Journal*

The making of criminals

- Schedule 26, Paragraph 18 (4) of the School Standards Framework Act 1998 makes it a criminal offence to 'wilfully obstruct an inspector conducting an inspection of a nursery'.

- Police can impose curfews on all under-16-year-olds between 9 p.m. and 6 a.m.

- Tahir Mahmood accidentally splashed a police officer while driving through a puddle. He apologised but Lancashire police and the Crown Prosecution Service charged him ('driving without consideration for other road users'). He was acquitted (court costs: £20,000).

- The power to detain suspected terrorists indefinitely was passed by Jack Straw when he was Home Secretary. He said at the time the power would be used only against people against whom there was a reasonable suspicion of terrorist activity. Subsequently, it has been used against antiwar protestors including an 11-year-old girl riding her bike, who objected to American bombers based in Britain being used in Iraq.

- Under the 2003 Sexual Offences Bill, two 15-year-olds deemed to have kissed or caressed in a sexual manner could face five years in prison.

- The parents who allow this to happen in their house could face 14 years in prison.

- David Blunkett, when he was the Home Secretary, suggested that all offences, including dropping litter, be deemed arrestable.

The government, in accordance with an EU directive, introduced a 'horse passport' in 2005 to identify every horse in
England, each with a distinctive silhouette. The purpose is
to document the medication given to any horse so that if it
is slaughtered for meat and entered into the human food
chain its chemistry can be monitored. This affects an
insignificant number of horses in Britain. The proposal that
only horses presented for slaughter be required to have a
passport was indignantly rejected.

Driven to despair

Stuck in traffic and 'barely moving', Stephen Lynch took his
hands off the steering wheel to brush his hair. He was given
a £30 fixed penalty by Peterborough and Cambridgeshire
police. He appealed. His prosecution took seven months to
come to court. He won. The prosecution failed to prove
their case beyond reasonable doubt.

Sarah McCaffrey was prosecuted for holding an apple
while turning left in her car. 'I wasn't speeding or swerving
around. It was a small apple and I had both hands on the
steering wheel when I turned into the road (in second gear).
The apple was in my right hand but I could still hold the
steering wheel and steer the car.'

Her lawyer told the court she had been driving in dry
conditions, that there was no traffic or pedestrians and that
the manoeuvre was carried out perfectly.

Northumbria Police used a helicopter, fixed-wing aircraft
and a video-equipped patrol car to gather evidence. She
was found guilty and fined £50 with £100 costs.

In 2000, Linda Smart of Calne, Wiltshire, was fined £40 for taking a sip of mineral water while sitting at traffic lights.

Lee Poole, 20, was fined £30 for eating a sausage roll as he waited in his car at a junction in Harrogate.

~

An inspector from the Cambridgeshire force wrote to the parents of a teenager who had been spotted smoking. Paul and Dawn Geer were warned that their son Karl, 15, risked becoming caught up in crime.

~

'Emma took Peter [her baby] to their GP because he had a lump on the side of his head. Although it didn't seem to be causing him any pain or affecting his behaviour, she wanted it checked out as she had no idea how it had got there ... A hairline crack was found in the skull. Since Emma couldn't explain the wound, the paediatrician deemed it suspicious and police and social services were summoned. They never left the hospital as a family. Peter was taken into care ... (and now lives with adopters, a situation which, when formalised, will be irreversible).

'The police dropped the matter, but social services pursued it. Emma and Martin [her husband] fear that their educated and reasoned approach counted against them. "They want you to admit guilt or blame one other and ask for help. We wouldn't do that, so we were considered in denial and beyond help."'

Cassandra Jardine, *Daily Telegraph*, 9 August 2004

The child's formal adoption came into effect a month later, even though medical evidence had come to light supporting the parents' case. (The family's names were changed in the article.)

∿

Parents of autistic children who raised £500,000 in government grants and from private sponsors opened a school for autistic children. It is a registered charity, was approved by the Department for Education and Skills and passed its preliminary Ofsted inspection. The local council, backed by the Special Educational Needs and Disability Tribunal, has found the school to be 'inappropriate' and threatened to prosecute the parents of any child sent there for encouraging their children's truancy.

∿

Small churches are closing because they cannot afford expensive building work needed for wheelchair ramps and lavatories for the disabled to comply with the Disability Discrimination Act. A spokesman for the Department for Work and Pensions insisted there was 'simply no need for any building to close'.

∿

After you've filled out a passport application you find you've done it in blue ink, not black, or you've misspelled a word at the end and you try to Tipp-Ex it out and the form is rejected because the witness's signature goes fractionally outside the signature box and it's the fifth form you've filled out and they won't accept photocopied documents or short birth certificates and your mother wasn't born in England before 1982 even though you were born in England but your father married another wife in 1996 and you have to attend the passport office personally in Petty France but they send you to Lunar House in Croydon and you are never seen again.

⁓

Between 1997 and the summer of 2004, Labour ministers created more than 600 new criminal offences.

⁓

The then new Judicial Appointments and Conduct Ombudsman would ensure the 'transparency' for appointments, said the Lord Chancellor. The identity of the judges convicted by the tribunal would be kept secret. In order to preserve public confidence in them and their judgements.

⁓

The Information Commissioner said there was a growing danger of an East German Stasi-style snooping if the state gathers too much information about individual citizens. He singled out three projects he believed were of particular concern. They are:

- [then Home Secretary] David Blunkett's identity card scheme.

- A separate population register planned by the Office of National Statistics.

- Proposals for a database of every child from birth to 18.

The population register will include all present and past addresses of individuals with their fingerprints. Police and HM Revenue and Customs will have access to the register. The Home Secretary will also be able to give any Whitehall department access without the need for a new Act of Parliament.

After detention without trial was declared illegal by the House of Lords, legal representatives of the Belmarsh detainees were warned that their clients might be sectioned under the Mental Health Act. It was true that many of the detainees did suffer mental health problems, largely through having been detained in solitary confinement for three years.

'Many Members [of Parliament] have gone nap on the issue. They voted, first, to abolish trial by jury in less serious cases; secondly to abolish trial by jury in more serious cases; thirdly, to approve an illegal war; fourthly to create a gulag at Belmarsh; and fifthly to lock up people in their homes. It is truly terrifying to imagine what those Members of Parliament will vote for next. I can describe all that only as New Labour's descent into hell.'

Brian Sedgemore MP, who defected from Labour just before the 2005 election

Under the rules, Australians, Canadians, New Zealanders, South Africans and Americans must prove they have a good grasp of English to become UK citizens. Under the new rules, all migrants wanting British passports must prove sufficient English knowledge, the easiest means to which is gaining an English for Speakers of Other Languages certificate.

Those who speak English as their first language cannot sign up, however – they need written confirmation from a designated person that they have an equivalent qualification. Proof can be obtained by having a chat with a designated person.

~

'Anyone who wishes to go to the US to work or study is required to set up an interview by dialling a £1.30 a minute premium telephone line, as though you are seeking hot lesbian sex.

'Then you join a queue outside the embassy at 7.30am. As it happens, the information I and my fellow queuers had got from the premium line turned out to be incorrect, so we had to leave the queue to find a bank, wait for an hour for it to open, pay in £60 for our visa fee, then rejoin the back of the queue.

'"Sorry about that," said the affable young man doing the crowd control in Grosvenor Square, "they're an outsourced private company who give out the wrong information to everyone."

'Seven hours after I joined the queue outside the embassy, I was summoned to be fingerprinted. "I'm glad to say, your application has been successful," the woman told me after inspecting my application form for 30 seconds, in a voice suggesting I had won the lottery. But of course I could not take my passport home with me. That cost another £10 for the courier, the only way you can get your passport back.'

Stephen Robinson, *Daily Telegraph*

In an evaluation of police performance, the Met scored highest in Strategic Management (134 out of 160) and lowest in Catching Criminals (93 out of 160).

'The evolution of man is based on extremely subjective interpretation, distortion and forgeries. In short, the evolution of man is a deception.'

Leaflet at Guy's Hospital in London produced by the Al-Nasr Trust

Mr Cook lived in Bristol with his disabled wife and their disabled daughter Freya (they both have multiple sclerosis). In August 2003, a group of late-night revellers attacked Mrs Cook with a bottle and a mobile phone outside the family home when she asked them to keep the noise down.

In the mêlée, Mrs Cook was being dragged around by the hair; Mr Cook hit one of the men with a hockey stick and managed to drag his wife and daughter indoors. When the gang forced their way into the house. Mr Cook drove them out with a spare stair spindle.

Two policemen arrived and arrested Mr Cook and his wife for actual bodily harm, along with one of the attackers. It was, said Mr Cook, 'a surreal experience'.

The charge against Mrs Cook was later dropped, but the charge against Mr Cook was upgraded to grievous bodily harm. Eighteen months later, he was acquitted at Bristol Crown Court.

~

'On taking possession of my new house I called BT to have the account changed to my name. The operator then asked whether I wanted a phone directory entry, to which I replied "no". When I asked what my number would be, I was told: "I'm sorry sir, we can't give out ex-directory numbers."'

Letter in *The Times*

~

Social services fads

- Anal dilatation.
- Satanic ritual abuse.
- Münchausen Syndrome by Proxy.
- Shaken-baby syndrome.

Sally Clarke was accused of killing her babies; her jury was told by expert witness Professor Sir Roy Meadow that the chance of the babies having died naturally was 73 million to one. She was found guilty and given a life sentence, partly as a result of the expert testimony. Sir Roy Meadow whose pet theory is Münchausen Syndrome by Proxy, (where mothers harm or kill their babies in order to attract attention to themselves) asserts that, unless proved otherwise, one cot death is a tragedy, two is suspicious and three is murder.

In Sally's case, the prosecution did not disclose the key findings of the lab report, which pointed to the presence of *Staphylococcus aureus* in two of the three babies who died. Two pathologists have said the *Staphylococcus aureus* infection was the most likely cause of death.

~

Professor Meadow's testimony led to the wrongful imprisonment of Angela Canning for 18 months following the death of her two children. He was paid £8,000 for his testimony; Angela Canning was paid nothing for her wrongful imprisonment.

~

A Euro-MP's staff member attended a rally for the European Constitution dressed as a monster with a sign round his neck saying, 'Devouring Democracy'. Security staff refused to let him into the European Parliament buildings until he obtained additional photo ID in which he was wearing the monster headgear.

~

The Proceeds of Crime Act (to stop money laundering) has been invoked in a divorce case and a precedent established. If family lawyers find any undeclared money they must report it to the National Crime Investigation Service.

The first duty of an accountant is no longer to his client but to the Revenue or Customs. If the accountant discovers his client is not paying as much tax as he or she should, the accountant is now required by law to inform on the client.

~

Privacy International says: British Telecom has established a system allowing it to keep records of our phone calls and website visits for seven years. The Home Office is negotiating for access to this information (under the Anti-Terrorism Act).

The Severn Area Rescue Association's request to the Lottery for £5,000 to replace the 14-year-old Land Rover used to launch its lifeboats, was turned down because it could not provide details of the social backgrounds of the people it rescued (disadvantaged groups favoured by the Lottery include asylum seekers, ethnic-minority communities, the young and the elderly). The Samaritans' bid for £300,000 to renovate a Sheffield factory to house its 120 workers was turned down while £360,000 was approved for the Network of Sex Work Projects.

The Financial Services Authority handbook is vast and almost incomprehensible – the only way to look at it is via the search engine on the FSA website as, apparently, 'if printed out it would stand nine feet high'.

Evidence to Lords Select Committee

New police officers no longer owe allegiance to the Crown (outside and above party politics), but to the government of the day (the reverse).

Is it legal to keep a baseball bat by the bed to use against intruders? A female reporter rang up the 43 police forces in England and Wales. Thirty-one said such actions could be or would be acceptable and ten said they would not. The remaining two offered a variety of verdicts.

Of the ten police forces, several said the keeping of a baseball bat by somebody who was not a baseball player was proof of 'premeditation' and 'intent to harm'. This was enough to justify prosecution.

An officer in the eastern area said, 'If someone came in and you knocked him out or did him some damage, you could well be charged with an offence and prosecuted.'

An officer in the western area said, 'You would end up being arrested – I can assure you of that.'

*

The Bill of Rights was written to limit the power of one individual, the king. These days, power has devolved down into an omnipresent administrative class. And it's out of control. The political class has reorganised itself, metastasised, into numberless autonomous cells (quangos, authorities, agencies, executives, tribunals). They have many functions but one principle: they're on a great civilising mission to replace our messy, superstitious, unhealthy, individualistic culture with theirs. Targets are issued, individual judgements overridden, all sorts of personal, professional and civic relationships are interrupted.

What is happening is a profoundly English phenomenon. Liberty is a great English tradition, but so is modernity.

That is our other ancestral characteristic. We led the world into the future with a flat legal regime, Parliament, a constitutional monarchy, a commercial revolution, the Reformation, the Industrial Revolution, democracy.

Modernity is what we're seeing now. Vast databases and state scrutiny of private behaviour – this is modernity in action.

I'm a pessimist. This isn't stoppable by any edict, new settlement or Bill of Rights. No new government is going to reverse the flow of power.

War

'And there was something in his [Jack Straw's] voice that made me think, 'God! They're going to invade Iraq!'

Independent sketch, two days after
11 September attack on New York

The evening after the attack on the World Trade Center, Bush was in the White House Situation Room. He saw his Counter-Terrorism Co-ordinator, Richard Clarke. He took him aside with a number of aides including Condoleezza Rice and according to Richard Clarke's memoir, Bush said, 'Go back over everything, everything. See if Saddam did this.'

And Clarke replied, 'But Mr President. Al Qaeda did this.' And Bush said, 'I know, I know but ... see if Saddam was involved. I want to know any shred.'

And when the President was told that no such link had been found either by the CIA or FBI before, Bush became,

'Testy.' He left the room with the third statement of his intentions: 'Look into Iraq, Saddam.'

~

'The very impossibility of questioning war because "it's not the decent thing to do" makes the play more of a personal tragedy. It is chiefly the tragedy of Stanhope ... Blair brought out the febrile character of Stanhope, wiring himself into his ever more circumscribed, troglodyte world ...'

> Fettes' school reviewer writing up pupil Tony Blair's
> performance in *Journey's End*

~

'Yesterday I came across a distraught family whose son had just been shot dead. "He was the driver of the deputy minister of health," his uncle said. "He just turned up as usual to drive him to work and there were gunmen waiting and they shot him dead. There was no news of this – and again, one must use the phrase 'of course' – on Iraq radio or television channel ..."'

> Robert Fisk, Baghdad, *Independent* February 2005

~

'I think all foreigners should stop interfering in the internal affairs of Iraq!'

> Paul Wolfowitz, US Deputy Secretary of Defence, July 2003

~

Perhaps the most insidious thing about Fox News is the ignorance it engenders. An opinion poll in October 2003 shows 33 per cent of Fox News viewers think the United

States has found weapons of mass destruction in Iraq, when it has not, and 67 per cent think Saddam Hussein had ties to al-Qaida, which the recently published 9/11 Commission report concluded he did not. The figures for listeners to National Public Radio, America's equivalent to Radio 4, were 11 per cent and 16 per cent respectively.

~

Erik Saar's report describes a military woman interrogating an unco-operative 21-year-old Saudi detainee at the Guantanamo Bay detention camp in Cuba. The interrogator wanted to "break him," according to Mr Saar's account, which added that the woman removed her uniform top to expose a tight-fitting T-shirt. She began taunting the detainee, the report says, touching her breasts, rubbing them against the prisoner's back and commenting on his apparent erection.

When asked how she could break the prisoner, a Muslim linguist told the woman to tell him she was menstruating, then to touch him and to turn off the water in his cell so he could not wash. 'The concept was to make the detainee feel that, after talking to her, he was unclean and was unable to go before his God in prayer and gain strength,' the report says.

~

'The truth is, the secret service is the worst in the world, the most inefficient, badly run, highly political outfit in the US government.'

Bill Gulley, former Director of the
White House Military Office

~

177

Outtake from Michael Moore's *Fahrenheit 9/11*, recorded a year before the interviewee's new appointment: 'I couldn't get a job with the CIA today. I am not qualified. I don't have the language skills ... I don't have the cultural background ... And I certainly don't have the technical skills.'

Porter Goss, new Head of the CIA

A retired army major, 54, who is deaf in one ear, has no sense of smell, and 'doesn't know one end of an SA80 assault rifle from another', was asked if he was prepared to serve in Iraq. Ned Middleton believed that the MoD might be trying to recruit a Dad's Army of reservists on the cheap. 'If they recruit people like me for six-month tours of duty they save money because that would be it for me after the tour. But if they recruit somebody in their early twenties they would have to pay them for however long their service was, find them a home and all the expense that goes with it.'

More than a quarter of the British troops sent to fight in Iraq had failed their basic weapons test. Senior officers had wanted training to start four months before the war was due to start, but the Ministry of Defence vetoed the request for fear of making known the fact that Britain had agreed to support President Bush's decision. Geoff Hoon, the then defence secretary, was wont to say that war was 'not inevitable'.

Lance Corporal Ian Blaymire was thus cleared of manslaughter after having shot and killed his friend, Sergeant John Nightingale. The judge said, 'Your training was deficient, you shouldn't have been deployed without further training. The system in Iraq was very slack in weapons-handling terms. You have been let down by the Army.'

'We may need to flatten Fallujah. We may need to destroy it. We may need to grind it, pulverise it and salt the soil ... Here's an opportunity to show that it doesn't pay to resort to barbarism and terrorism.'

Joseph Farah, American journalist

Adnan Pachachi, Iraq's elder statesman, after meeting Saddam Hussein in the latter's prison cell: 'I then asked him why did he kill so many people, why he had been such a ruthless ruler. And he said, "Iraq needs a just but a firm ruler." I said, "You were not a just ruler. You were in fact an oppressive ruler, an oppressive tyrant over the Iraqi people." And he said: "You know, sometimes one has to use force in order to keep the peace and unity and integrity of the country."'

Donald MacIntyre, Independent

Blown!

Valerie Plame was married to US Ambassador Joseph Wilson. He was sent to Iraq to find out whether Saddam Hussein was procuring uranium from Niger. When he found that the claim was bogus, and outraged that his government was taking the country into war on the basis of a lie, he wrote an article in the *New York Times*. In retaliation, administration officials revealed that his wife was a covert CIA operative.

Katherine Gun worked as a translator at the UK government's communications headquarters GCHQ. She was arrested, accused of breaching the Official Secrets Act. She was sacked in 2003, but at her trial no evidence was offered against her by the government. She revealed an email from US spies asking British counterparts to tap the telephones of UN Security Council members.

~

Asked if it was inconceivable that the world would support US military action against Iran, presumably bombings or using Israel as a 'proxy', Foreign Secretary Jack Straw replied, 'Not only is that inconceivable but I think the prospect of it happening is inconceivable.'

4 November 2004

The *New Yorker* magazine reported that teams of US special forces had infiltrated Iran to scout suspected weapons sites that would be targeted in future air strikes. Seymour Hersh, the magazine's award-winning journalist, quoted a US official as saying that after Afghanistan and Iraq 'we're going to have the Iranian campaign'.

18 January 2005

~

The elections in Iraq were so dangerous that international observers observed them from another country.

~

A study by the Royal Institute of International Affairs asserts that Western intelligence's success in predicting Soviet moves was no better than that of America's think tanks.

'Sergei Konrashov, a retired KGB chief of counter-intelligence, told me [Philip Knightley of the *Sunday Times*] at a conference in Germany that if the KGB was forced to choose between a Russian mole in the US administration and a subscription to the *New York Times*, he would take the *New York Times* any day.'

'Sir Peter Heap, a former British ambassador, described the MI6 reports leaving his embassy as "commonly little more than gossip and tittle-tattle, frequently so at variance with the facts that we knew them to have little or no credibility."

'Sir Peter once spotted that the MI6 officer in his embassy had simply copied a report almost word for word from the local newspaper, sending it to London dressed up as "intelligence from a well-placed source".

'Their verdict (high-level consumers of intelligence in the MoD and Foreign Office) is uncomfortable. The spies are good at tactical intelligence. They did extremely well in Northern Ireland, almost certainly making the key difference in the struggle with the IRA. But at the grand strategic level, says a former assistant chief of the defence staff, it has now become clear that the intelligence services know little more than the average Sunday newspaper reader. '

Andrew Gilligan, *Spectator*, May 2004

'The allegation that the 45-minute claim [concerning the readiness for use of WMD] provoked disquiet among the intelligence community, which disagreed with its inclusion in the dossier ... is also completely and totally untrue.'

Tony Blair, House of Commons, 4 June 2003

Brian Jones of the Defence Intelligence Staff wrote memos explicitly expressing disquiet, and more.

Also: 'This 45-minute shit' – CIA Chief, George Tenet, quoted in the Butler report

~

'There was no attempt, at any time, by any official, or minister, or member of number 10 Downing Street staff, to override the intelligence judgements of the Joint Intelligence Committee.

Tony Blair, House of Commons, 4 June 2003

However, Jonathan Powell: 'I think the statement on page 19 that "Saddam is able to use chemical and biological weapons if he believes his regime is under threat" is a bit of a problem. It backs up the ... argument that there is no CBW [chemical and biological warfare] threat and we will only create one if we attack him. I think you should redraft the para.'

~

'I did not authorise the leaking of the name of David Kelly. Emphatically not. That is completely untrue.'

Tony Blair, press conference, 22 July 2003

He chaired the meeting that authorised the 'naming strategy' for David Kelly. He also told Lord Hutton's inquiry, '... responsibility is mine in the end. I take the decisions.'

'We made great efforts to ensure Dr Kelly's anonymity'

Defence Secretary Geoff Hoon, BBC interview, 19 July 2003

~

However, to Lord Hutton: 'If a journalist approached the press office with the right name, then that name would be confirmed by press officers.'

When Hoon was asked why he hadn't corrected the interpretation of the '45-minute claim' in the dossier (that the weapons could attack British troops as far afield as Cyprus), he told Hutton he hadn't seen the headlines. He had been in Poland that day.

*

'[Tory leader] Mr [Michael] Howard quoted from the latest report: "Little was known about Saddam's WMD pro-gramme since 1998", but the Prime Minister told us it was "beyond doubt he continued to make WMD". How can he maintain he accurately reported the intelligence?"

'Mr Blair didn't misrepresent the intelligence: he took great care to receive intelligence that was already misrepresented. Mr Blair didn't debauch the intelligence, he didn't even debauch the intelligence officers. Others did that dark work for him, maybe without even being told to.

'There was a case for going to war against Saddam but it wasn't the case the Prime Minister presented to us. The weaponry wasn't "beyond doubt", the threat wasn't "serious and current", nor was evidence for active weapons "detailed and grave". Professional caveats and cautions had been stripped away, and the intelligence described as solid and comprehensive was later revealed to have been "sporadic, patchy and limited".

'But, as I say, Mr Blair has taken great care not to lie to us. He didn't tell the truth but he didn't lie. He arranged matters in such a way that he would never hear anything that contradicted the case for war. He is a lawyer, remember, but more than that, a barrister. Mr Blair used his ministers, civil servants, special advisers as barristers use solicitors, to give him the brief, to tell him the things he needed to justify war. That's why he didn't know that the 45-minute weapons were pop-guns and not ballistic missiles. He didn't ask. He didn't want to know. His colleagues knew he didn't want to know. They all collaborated in the Prime Minister's vast, willed ignorance.

'I hope you are reassured.'

Independent sketch

'Again, the Prime Minister had his sad face on. He began PMQs with it. He was grieving for families of soldiers killed in Iraq. He grieves a lot these days, it's surprising he gets anything else done. Maybe you can process grief more efficiently if you practise. Perhaps he's got a book. *Ten Grieving Tips For Busy People*. When you're Prime Minister so much time is taken up providing the tools to allow people to choose the skills programmes to fulfil their potential in community partnerships and lifelong learning. There's not the luxury to spend looking at the wall and folding and refolding your hands wondering why your son died. There's not the leisure to remember your little one as a five-year-old going "Bang! Bang!" in the back garden, or pushing him around in a wheelbarrow on summer evenings.

'Julian Brazier is a gangling, good hearted, soldierly sort of fellow. He referred to these servicemen who'd given their lives so that elections might be held in Iraq. He asked the prime minister why "when he'd found time to drop a line to Ozzy Osbourne who fell off his quad bike" he hadn't found time to write to or visit any of these afore-mentioned families. The words "Ozzy Osbourne" were very effective in this context. As were "quad bike".

'"I'm sorry he makes that point in those terms," the Prime Minister replied, provoking an odd, snorting noise from parts of his audience. "We grieve for the families," he went on, "we give them every support, everyone in this House does. That is the case for myself." Well, not quite every support. American families are to get half a million dollars for their bereavement. Here, Mr Brazier suggested, they don't get so much as a visit from a minister. Maybe the government doesn't want "to intrude on their grief". But then nothing's ever prevented them intruding before, there must be another explanation.'

Independent sketch

The British government – which partially justifies its war in Iraq on the grounds of Saddam Hussein's monstrosities – is not providing evidence for his trial on the grounds that it breaches his human rights.

In 2006 Defence Secretary Dr John Reid said he hoped the British army would go to Afghanistan and return 'without a shot being fired'. In 2007, four million rounds were fired by the British. Dr Reid has found a £50,000 job working for G4S Security Services, a company that provides training for army units sending troops to Afghanistan.

HUTTON
REPORT

I Got My Rights! (I Got Yours, Too!)

Human rights cases have included:

- A robber winning £1,000 damages because police breached his right to privacy by filming him to gain evidence.
- An aggressive beggar getting legal aid to claim her rights to freedom of movement had been breached when magistrates banned her from a city centre.
- A paedophile who won funds to sue the government for making prison life too boring.
- A schoolboy suing his head teacher after being suspended for allegedly setting the school on fire.
- AIDS sufferers from overseas who have used the Act to make it almost impossible for them to be deported to a country with a worse healthcare system.

'When I started a new job, running a small arts organisation, James had no trouble tracking me down. By this time –

seven years after I'd first met him – the messages were abusive. He hoped, he said, that my babies would die of acid poisoning since I had denied him the chance to have any of his own. And then he saw our ad for an administrative assistant, and applied for the job. In his letter of application he said that he should be running the organisation, or perhaps the Foreign Office.

'A few weeks later, after the appointment had been successfully made and the 83 unsuccessful candidates had been informed, I got a letter from the Regional Secretary for Employment Tribunals. I had been accused, it informed me, of disability discrimination. I almost laughed. I wrote a long letter outlining the history [of his stalking] and sent it, with witness statements from former colleagues and copies of letters and poems he'd sent. I got a terse note back advising me to "seek legal advice".

'"I'm afraid he's got a case," said the lawyer on our board. "Since you knew he had schizophrenia he can argue that you knowingly discriminated against someone with a disability. Welcome," he added with a dry laugh, "to the world of European law."'

Christina Patterson, *Independent,* 19 August 2004

~

'The burden of out-of-hours calls at night and the weekends has become steadily more onerous – increasing five-fold over the last 25 years. People are certainly no sicker than they were a quarter of a century ago – so this can only mean the sensible threshold for calling out a doctor has fallen ... More recently, patients have cottoned onto more subtle ways of getting their doctor out of bed by hinting at symptoms that suggest some really serious illness such as meningitis. "His head hurts and he can't stand the light." By the time the doctor arrives the child is sleeping peacefully ... In these litigious times the price for "failing to visit" can be very high indeed.'

James Le Fanu, *Daily Telegraph*

The tide may be on the turn ...

Ukla Heywood, 21, sued the Duke of Edinburgh Award scheme after suffering from sore feet following a 50-mile trek in the Lake District. District judge Peter Bullock threw the claim out at Newcastle County Court: 'This was intended to be a test of physical strength,' he said.

A senior judge disallowed a claim for damages by a girl who had broken her arm ten years before at her primary school. She had recovered and continued to succeed at women's football. Lauren Babbings, suing at the age of 17, was given legal aid to sue her local authority. Lord Justice Brooke said, 'How boring it would be if there were no risk.'

A coroner in October 2004 refused to find fault with Sainsbury's after hearing how Alfred Neave, a retired architect, died last August after tripping over a box left on the floor. Dr Paul Knapman, sitting at Westminster's coroner's court, said he did not wish to further restrict our 'over-ordered' society. 'When all is said and done, it is up to each individual to keep a lookout.'

'The distress call from the mobile phone of a couple stranded up a mountain in the Lake District sounded serious. "We are lost in the mist," said an anxious voice. "My wife is very frightened. Please come and find us." As the message continued, the mountain rescue team listened incredulously. "And could you send a helicopter?" asked the caller. "We have a dinner date at 7pm, which we really don't want to miss."

'Stuart Hulse, who has been a mountain rescuer for nearly 40 years, can tell many more stories like this. Such as the recent case of a group of 11 professionals on a management bonding weekend who rang claiming to be lost in a valley. The mountain rescuers were scrambled and found them in 20 minutes. It transpired that, although the group had gone slightly out of its way, they had no transport and wanted to be driven back to their accommodation.

'"When I started climbing and fell walking, self-reliance was the name of the game," says Hulse, 69. "There was a bit of a stigma if you had to be rescued because you took pride in being prepared and having the equipment to confront the elements ... Most of the time any trouble people get into is down to their own recklessness and incompetence. And yet many don't even seem embarrassed about it."'

Carol Midgely, *The Times*

In the year to April 2004 employment tribunal cases increased by 17 per cent. One company reported that CCTV caught a worker falling off his bike outside the factory gates, then getting back on again and falling off inside in order to claim compensation from his employer.

Fruit, Nuts and Other Annoyances

Trading-standards officers found that Tesco's Kid's Pizza, publicised as 'controlled sodium', contained ten times the amount of salt allowed for foods claiming to be 'reduced salt'. There is no standard definition of 'controlled'.

∿

A Tesco's cereal with 'controlled sugar' was almost one-third sugar.

∿

Dr Michael Roizen, the inventor of the RealAge concept, says he has identified 78 'key behaviours and clinical indicators', which reveal how fast our bodies are ageing. His calendar age 55 but his 'real age' is 39. To find out your 'real age' you can pay Dr Roizen £1,500.

∿

Lee Stuart Evans and his wife Stephanie left their academic jobs as research biologists (combined salary: £18,000) to be window cleaners (earnings: £50,000).

Molecular biologist Dr Karl Gensberg doubled his salary by ditching his £23,000-a-year job to become a plumber.

~

This doesn't sound like a recorded message at first:

'Hi there. My name is David Williams. I'm calling you because one of my colleagues has been trying to get hold of you because someone in your household entered our draw last year and we've been trying to let you know you've won a major prize. Now, basically, you've either won two first-class return flights to New York, a Spanish cruise, £5,000 in cash or a BMW coupe. Now, to claim, you can write to me at our London ... no, actually, it's getting near the closing date so it might be better for you to call our 24-hour claim line ...'

Claim-line calls cost £1.50 a minute and lack conciseness: '... Now let's get down to details and find out what you've got. By calling us you've alerted our computers who may just need to check your award. You'll need a pen to take down your award number but don't worry, we'll repeat it, and it's been designed with you in mind to be easy to remember, because we want you to get your reward ...'

~

A Dutch artist was convicted by a French court for taking pictures of her naked children that were deemed to be obscene. Art experts denounced the prosecution of Kiki

Lamers, 40, whose work has an international following. She was given an eight-month suspended sentence and fined £3,000 for corrupting minors.

Ms Lamers, who paints stylised portraits of children from photographs, has held shows in Amsterdam and New York, and sells paintings for up to £11,000.

~

'Mr [Peter] Hain [MP] said in one breath he wanted to make the place accessible to young people and in the next he accused the Tories of losing the elections last week. Young people might think the Tories, with their larger share of the vote and the increased number of seats they'd won and the larger number of councils under their control, these young people might be thinking the Tories won the elections last week. They would have to grapple with Mr Hain's explanation that he was taking into account the seasonally adjusted, regionally weighted results, balanced for this point in the electoral cycle and measured against second-preference expectations. The result was the opposite, young people would find. Young people, of course, might prefer to watch mud wrestling, for its elevated sense of professional ethics.'

Independent sketch

~

Euro target from one of the Euro-summits was declared: Europe was 'to become the most dynamic economy in the world by 2010'.

Growth and productivity has fallen and unemployment has risen. (It is higher in Germany than at any time since

Adolf Hitler came to power and in the EU it totals 19 million.)

A bank robber was allowed to claim the £1,400 cost of the gun he used as a legitimate business expense, set against the gross proceeds of £4,700, which he stole in the southern Dutch town of Chaam. Jailing him for four years, the judge at Breda criminal court reduced his fine by that amount. The Dutch prosecutors' service said that the judge had followed sound legal precedents.

The economist Lord Skidelsky failed a Russian economy paper when he took an A-level in Russian. The examination board said that his points were irrelevant, and that people who had too much knowledge of a subject often over-answered a question.

From his garden, army veteran Charles Mayall confronted yobs in the street outside. One jumped over his front gate and hit him with a piece of wood. Police found Mr Mayall and the other man on the ground. Mr Mayall was arrested along with his attacker and spent eight hours in a cell without being allowed a solicitor or doctor (he had a broken thumb and bruised ribs). He was charged with assault (he had broken his attacker's jaw). After three court appearances and five months, the charge of assault was dropped on grounds of insufficient evidence.

Inspector Jerry Butler said Mr Mayall had to be arrested because of his 'conduct'. The man restrained by Mr Mayall was charged with criminal damage.

~

Migrants seeking permission to stay in Britain have to be able to demonstrate language ability to be able to communicate. Dr Kimberley Fisher (an American academic) was turned down three times by the Immigration Department in Liverpool because of 'the law regarding knowledge of English'. The letter sent with it said that a GCSE in English would be proof enough. She wrote back enclosing her PhD certificate and was rejected again. After the intervention of a junior Home Office minister, Professor Kimberley was rejected a third time. Dame Bridget Ogilvie (who ran Britain's biggest healthcare charity) was born in Australia and was denied a passport because she had not sat the English test.

~

In 2004 the Law Lords declared that detention without trial for foreign nationals was disproportionate and discriminatory. The Home Office resolved the question of discrimination with a law making it apply to British nationals as well.

~

In 2000, Chancellor Gordon Brown wrote off more than £30 million owed by Uganda. In the same month, the president of Uganda announced the order of an executive jet – at a cost of over £30 million.

EU

According to EU regulations, the only legal way of disposing of Scottish sewage pellets is by burning them in special incinerators designed to serve no useful purpose such as generating electricity (the pellets are classified as 'waste' not 'fuel').

In European Standing Committee B they scrutinised the European Union draft budget. It took them a little less than an hour and a half. One Tory attended. He is fiercely Euro-sceptic. But because he wasn't a committee member he couldn't vote. He made the point that whatever the committee thought of the budget it wouldn't matter because the deal would done by the Prime Minister late at night in some smoke-free room in some EU budget conference. 'We have to struggle to pretend we are scrutinising it,' he said. That was true. The absent Tory committee members must have been struggling even harder to scrutinise it from a distance.

'"Every month I look at my payslip," an official told me, "and I try to work out how my net salary can be so much larger than my gross salary."

- EU officials pay a flat tax of 16 per cent.
- They receive an "expatriation allowance" equal to 16 per cent of their salary.
- Londoners working for the EU in London receive a weighting allowance of 39 per cent.
- Free medical insurance.
- Pension of up to 70 per cent of final salary.
- Subsidy for every dependent child.

'Three quarters of the MEPs in the current parliament are new. Yet when we met for the first time last month, we found dozens of pieces of legislation waiting for us. These bills have been drawn up by the parliament's secretariat, which will now steer them through with only minimal interference from Euro-MPs ...'

Daniel Hannan, Conservative MEP
for South East England

'One neglected aspect of the fact that the [EU] Council works in an open and transparent way is that the really important compromises and discussions are referred to lunches or dinners or the meals that the ministers have together. So we will put on weight! The official meetings don't last that long but the lunches are three or four or even more hours from now on.'

Commissioner Margaret Wallstrom's blog,
13 January 2005

'... a television station called Euronews. It is quite a decent channel offering news and sports in several languages. But when it reports directly on the EU, impartiality goes out of the window and we are treated to Soviet-style items about millions of workers waking up to higher standards thanks to the Commission. I found the contrast suspicious so I put down a written question asking Romano Prodi whether he gave Euronews any money. His reply was beyond parody. Yes, he said, he did give it grants, but such grants "in no way restrict the editorial freedom of the beneficiary who must, however, respect the image of the European institutions and the *raison d'être* and general objectives of the Union".'

Daniel Hannan, Conservative MEP
for South East England

Hans-Martin Tillack was investigating the Eurostat scandal, in which, allegedly, millions of euros have been diverted from the budget by Commission officials. Then he started to investigate the failure of EU authorities to act on tip-offs.

He was seized, questioned for ten hours without a lawyer, his computer and records and bank statements were confiscated. The raid was ordered by OLAF, the European Union's anti-corruption unit.

Deloitte has estimated the annual fraud in the Commission's administration of the European Union between 1997 and 2005 to be €8 billion.

'Since then,' writes Jens-Peter Bonde, MEP, 'there have been fewer cases, but the amounts involved have been larger. The numbers may even be much worse, but we cannot tell: no control authority has had a full overview.

- The Court of Auditors cannot obtain all documents.
- The mediator does not have the right to see all documents.
- The budgetary control committee in the EU Parliament is only superficially informed.

'Through 25 years I have, as member of the EU Parliament, asked for basic information on the use of EU funds. I have never had any serious answers on, for instance, the distribution of agricultural subsidies or on the number of working groups and their participants.'

∿

Parliament's European Scrutiny Committee sits in secret.

∿

Paul van Buitenen, the European Union official whose 1999 whistle-blowing revelations sparked the resignation of the entire European Commission, was demoted and had his salary halved. Three years later he returned to his native Netherlands, saying the pressure in Brussels had become too great to bear. The people whose 'corruption, cronyism and abuse of power' formed the basis of his whistle-blowing have all been confirmed in office or promoted.

∿

Marta Andreasen, the chief accountant for the European Union, refused to sign off the €69 billion accounts, declaring that the Commission's bookkeeping and general accounting procedures were 'chaotic' and 'shambolic'. They failed to detect negligence and inefficiency, and opened up the possibility of fraud. She was immediately suspended and banned from the building.

∿

Triumph of political language: it means what it seems to mean and at the same time seems to mean the opposite.

Former Tory chancellor Ken Clarke remarked in Parliament that he (pro-EU constitution) and David Heathcote-Amory (anti) – both experienced, intelligent, honourable individuals – couldn't agree what the con-stitution is trying to say with the words 'united ever more closely'.

∿

The constitution represents

'Thus far and no further on European integration'.

Foreign Secretary Jack Straw

'The birth certificate of the United States of Europe'.

Hans Martin Bury, German Minister for Europe

'A single European state bound by one European constitution'.

Joschka Fischer, German Foreign Minister

∿

A secret Treasury analysis of the single currency written in 1971 informed the then Prime Minister Edward Heath that monetary union 'has revolutionary long-term implications, both economic and political. It could imply the ultimate creation of a European federal state with a single currency. All the basic instruments of national economic policy – fiscal, monetary, incomes and regional policies – would be handed over to the central federal authorities.'

'There are some in this country who fear that in going into Europe we shall in some way sacrifice independence and sovereignty.' Heath said in a television broadcast on Britain's entry into the Common Market, January 1973, 'These fears, I need hardly say, are completely unjustified.'

A Scottish Office memo (9 November 1970) reported that ministers were being told how important it was not to get drawn into detailed explanations of just what problems might lie ahead for the fishermen because, 'in the wider UK context, they must be regarded as expendable'.

'The figure of 3.5 million jobs came from a report commissioned in 1999 by Britain in Europe from a reputable research organisation, the National Institute for Economic and Social Research.

'What the report actually stated was something very different. It did estimate that 3.5 million UK jobs were linked to trade with the EU. But even if Britain were to leave the EU, it pointed out, few of those jobs would disappear, because we would continue trading with the EU much as we do now (and as do other non-EU countries, such as Norway and Switzerland). But no sooner did Britain in Europe receive the report than it put out a press release claiming that "British withdrawal would cost 3.5 million jobs".

'The NIESR's director, Dr Martin Weale, was so angry at this misuse of his report that he described Britain in Europe's behaviour as "pure Goebbels".

'"We know that nine out of ten people will not have read the Constitution and will vote on the basis of what politicians and journalists say. More than that, if the answer is No, the vote will probably have to be done again, because it absolutely has to be Yes."'

Jean-Luc Dehaene, former Belgian Prime Minister and Vice-President of the EU Convention

It is said to be a myth that the EU promotes daft rules such as demanding 'straight bananas'.

It is, in fact, EU Regulation 2257/94 that requires that bananas to be at least 13.97cm long and 2.69cm round and do not have 'abnormal curvature', as set out in an eight-page directive drawn up in 1994.

(It's also true that this was originally an industry standard that was taken over by the EU and applied to the zone.)

'The only thing the British have ever given European farming is mad cow.'

Jacques Chirac

'The Union shall work for sustainable development of Europe based on balanced economic growth and price stability, a highly competitive social market economy, aiming at full employment and social progress, and with a high level of protection and improvement of the quality of the environment. It shall promote scientific and technological advance.'

European Constitution

Questions arising from this paragraph on which a Supreme Court would have to adjudicate:

- What is sustainable development?
- What is economic growth balanced between?
- At what point does inflation become unconstitutional?
- How high is highly competitive?
- What is a social market?
- If social considerations conflict with competition issues, which will take constitutional precedence across Europe?
- What is full employment?
- What is social progress? Who will define it?
- If the quality of the environment is to be improved, how will it be measured?
- How will scientific advance be promoted? Will it be unconstitutional not to promote it?

A number of French ideas on the relationship between citizen and society:

'L'état, c'est moi.' Louis XIV

'The general will rules in society as the private will governs each separate individual.' Robespierre

'Whoever refuses to obey the general shall be compelled to do so by the whole of society, which means nothing more or less than that he will be compelled to be free.' Rousseau

'I am myself the people.' Robespierre, after Louis XIV

Now the European Commission has recreated the idea first articulated by Louis XIV and Robespierre: it describes itself as 'the institution whose vocation is the completely impartial representation of the general interest'.

~

The next eight pages contain Euro-legislation. They are summed up in the 26 words at the end:

Article 1

Draft European legislative acts sent to the European Parliament and to the Council shall be forwarded to national Parliaments. For the purposes of this Protocol, "draft European legislative acts" shall mean proposals from the Commission, initiatives from a group of Member States, initiatives from the European Parliament, requests from the Court of Justice, recommendations from the European Central Bank and requests from the European Investment Bank for the adoption of a European legislative act.

Article 2

Draft European legislative acts originating from the Commission shall be forwarded to national Parliaments directly by the Commission, at the same time as to the European Parliament and the Council. Draft European legislative acts originating from the European Parliament shall be forwarded to national Parliaments directly by the European Parliament. Draft European legislative acts originating from a group of Member States, the Court of Justice, the European Central Bank or the European Investment Bank shall be forwarded to national Parliaments by the Council.

Article 3

National Parliaments may send to the Presidents of the European Parliament, the Council and the Commission a reasoned opinion on whether a draft European legislative act complies with the principle of subsidiarity, in accordance with the procedure laid down in the Protocol on the application of the principles of subsidiarity and proportionality. If the draft European legislative act originates from a group of Member States, the President of the Council shall forward the reasoned opinion or opinions to the governments of those Member States. If the draft European legislative act originates from the Court of Justice, the European Central Bank or the European Investment Bank, the President of the Council shall forward the reasoned opinion or opinions to the institution or body concerned.

Article 4

A six-week period shall elapse between a draft European legislative act being made available to national Parliaments in the official languages of the Union and the date when it is placed on a provisional agenda for the Council for its adoption or for adoption of a position under a legislative procedure. Exceptions shall be possible in cases of urgency, the reasons for which shall be stated in the act or position of the Council. Save in urgent cases for which due reasons have been given, no agreement may be reached on a draft European legislative act during those six weeks. Save in urgent cases for which due reasons have been given, a ten-day period shall elapse between the placing of a draft European legislative act on the provisional agenda for the Council and the adoption of a position.

Article 5

The agendas for and the outcome of meetings of the Council, including the minutes of meetings where the Council is deliberating on draft European legislative acts, shall be forwarded directly to national Parliaments, at the same time as to Member States' governments.

Article 6

When the European Council intends to make use of Article IV-444(1) or (2) of the Constitution, national Parliaments shall be informed of the initiative of the European Council at least six months before any European decision is adopted.

Article 7

The Court of Auditors shall forward its annual report to national Parliaments, for information, at the same time as to the European Parliament and to the Council.

Article 8

Where the national Parliamentary system is not unicameral, Articles 1 to 7 shall apply to the component chambers.

Article 9

The European Parliament and national Parliaments shall together determine the organisation and promotion of effective and regular interparliamentary co-operation within the Union.

Article 10

A conference of Parliamentary Committees for Union Affairs may submit any contribution it deems appropriate for the attention of the European Parliament, the Council and the Commission. That conference shall in addition promote the exchange of information and best practice between national Parliaments and the European Parliament, including their special committees. It may also organise interparliamentary conferences on specific topics, in particular to debate matters of common foreign and security policy, including common security and defence policy. Contributions from the conference shall not bind national Parliaments and shall not prejudge their positions.

214 Part IV

2. Protocol on the application of the principles of subsidiarity and proportionality.

The high contracting parties, wishing to ensure that decisions are taken as closely as possible to the citizens of the Union, resolved to establish the conditions for the application of the principles of subsidiarity and proportionality, as laid down in Article I-11 of the Constitution, and to establish a system for monitoring the application of those principles, have agreed upon the following provisions, which shall be annexed to the Treaty establishing a Constitution for Europe:

Article 1

Each institution shall ensure constant respect for the principles of subsidiarity and proportionality, as laid down in Article I-11 of the Constitution.

Article 2

Before proposing European legislative acts, the Commission shall consult widely. Such consultations shall, where appropriate, take into account the regional and local dimension of the action envisaged. In cases of exceptional urgency, the Commission shall not conduct such consultations. It shall give reasons for its decision in its proposal.

Article 3

For the purposes of this Protocol, "draft European legislative acts" shall mean proposals from the Commission, initiatives from a group of Member States, initiatives from the European Parliament, requests from the Court of Justice, recommendations from the European Central Bank and requests from the European Investment Bank for the adoption of a European legislative act.

Article 4

The Commission shall forward its draft European legislative acts and its amended drafts to national Parliaments at the same time as to the Union legislator. The European Parliament shall forward its draft European legislative acts and its amended drafts to national Parliaments.

The Council shall forward draft European legislative acts originating from a group of Member States, the Court of Justice, the European Central Bank or the European Investment Bank and amended drafts to national Parliaments. Upon adoption, legislative resolutions of the European Parliament and positions of the Council shall be forwarded by them to national Parliaments.

Article 5

Draft European legislative acts shall be justified with regard to the principles of subsidiarity and proportionality. Any draft European legislative act should contain a detailed statement making it possible to appraise compliance with the principles of subsidiarity and proportionality. This statement should contain some assessment of the proposal's financial impact and, in the case of a European framework law, of its implications for the rules to be put in place by Member States, including, where necessary, the regional legislation. The reasons for concluding that a Union objective can be better achieved at Union level shall be substantiated by qualitative and, wherever possible, quantitative indicators. Draft European legislative acts shall take account of the need for any burden, whether financial or administrative, falling upon the Union, national governments, regional or local authorities, economic operators and citizens, to be minimised and commensurate with the objective to be achieved.

Article 6

Any national Parliament or any chamber of a national Parliament may, within six weeks from the date of transmission of a draft European legislative act, send to the Presidents of the European Parliament, the Council and the Commission a reasoned opinion stating why it considers that the draft in question does not comply with the principle of subsidiarity. It will be for each national Parliament or each chamber of a national Parliament to consult, where appropriate, regional parliaments with legislative powers. If the draft European legislative act originates from a group of Member States, the President of the Council shall forward the opinion to the governments of those Member States. If the draft European legislative act originates from the Court of Justice, the European Central

Bank or the European Investment Bank, the President of the Council shall forward the opinion to the institution or body concerned.

Article 7

The European Parliament, the Council and the Commission, and, where appropriate, the group of Member States, the Court of Justice, the European Central Bank or the European Investment Bank, if the draft legislative act originates from them, shall take account of the reasoned opinions issued by national Parliaments or by a chamber of a national Parliament. Each national Parliament shall have two votes, shared out on the basis of the national Parliamentary system. In the case of a bicameral Parliamentary system, each of the two chambers shall have one vote. Where reasoned opinions on a draft European legislative act's non-compliance with the principle of subsidiarity represent at least one third of all the votes allocated to the national Parliaments in accordance with the second paragraph, the draft must be reviewed. This threshold shall be a quarter in the case of a draft European legislative act submitted on the basis of Article III-264 of the Constitution on the area of freedom, security and justice.

Part IV

After such review, the Commission or, where appropriate, the group of Member States, the European Parliament, the Court of Justice, the European Central Bank or the European Investment Bank, if the draft European legislative act originates from them, may decide to maintain, amend or withdraw the draft. Reasons must be given for this decision.

Those previous 1,500 words mean the following: When member countries object to an EU proposal, the EU will have to consider the objection. It won't, however, be obliged to do anything about it.

⁓

There was a short but very sharp row on the radio among a panel of Euros and Neuros. Half the panellists were in favour of the European Constitution (whatever it turns out to be) and the other half were against it (whatever it turns out to be). The logic of each position turned out to be an unreliable guide as to what we should think. Both positions are solidly based on entirely romantic premises.

The Euros believe that ever closer integration will create a pan-European political class that will lead the continent into an era of peace and prosperity. The Neuros believe that there is a British way of doing things that is superior to and quite at odds with Continental habits. This latter idea is so susceptible to mockery that its adherents never quite come out and put it like that. Let us overcome, if we can, our fear of being labelled Little Englanders, racists, xenophobes, incipient fascists and national triumphalists and assert straightforwardly: the British are different.

Put like that, it's uncontroversial. How can we be described as anything else? Our language is different from any other in Europe, and language moulds a way of thinking. Our public services deliver different standards of care and achievement from anywhere else in Europe, that is widely accepted. The way our media treat our leaders is entirely different, and so is the way our young people behave on holiday. No other girls fall out of their brassieres by accident; no other European youth rut so drunkenly in public. The whole march of our history and culture runs at a different angle from that of Continental Europe's. The British empire was run on very different lines from the French or German empires and, for better and worse, with very different results.

However, there is some convergence; that, too, is uncontroversial. Observation confirms that we can buy Head 'n' Shoulders in Prague. Roads and roundabouts are constructed in the same way throughout the Continent; sometimes we can hardly tell whether we're driving into Brussels or Milan. Independent central banks are producing similar interest rates. A political consensus (who knows how long it will last?) seems to be settling over the whole area – leftish in social affairs, rightish in economic terms. Euro-politicians are producing legislation to make a more homogeneous Europe. Maybe they will succeed; they've certainly succeeded so far.

Life has changed a lot over the last generation. The state has made and continues to make very significant gains at the expense of civilian liberty.

Yes, the increase in the power of the political class since 1970 has constituted a silent revolution, a putsch, almost, by the clerks, the technocrats, the wonks. The massive increase in regulation has been essential to the European project but is also quite at odds with, as we shall have to call it sooner or later, the British way of doing things. And here we arrive at the controversial point. Does the British way of doing things exist, and, if it does, should we stop it?

The British character has a wild strand in it, we see it in ourselves and, in modified forms, in all the old Commonwealth countries. It is an almost anarchic energy that is regularly released in one of two ways: under licence in our Saturnalian rituals (sporting, very often, or alcoholic); or less formally by establishing the largest empire of its time, creating an industrial revolution or facing down the established power of the state.

Which brings us to the central proposition. This refusal to subjugate oneself entirely to the established power of the state found its original legal expression in Magna Carta. This founding document for Britain set out a direction very different from Giscard d'Estaing's founding document for Europe.

Magna Carta's purpose then was exactly opposite to the European constitution's now – it was drafted not to *create* state power but to *limit* the power of the state. And its vitality over the next 500 years was palpable. It was reissued in 1225; it was reconfirmed in 1297 when Edward I was forced to bow to its terms. It contributed to the Peasants' Revolt (when peasants claimed the freedom to move around and sell their scarce labour). It animated the Levellers and the Cromwellian revolution. It inspired, for goodness' sake, the American constitution.

As Danny Danziger and John Gillingham tell us in their book *1215: The Year of Magna Carta*, 'All this seventeenth-century fuss meant that Magna Carta was headline news at the time the American colonies were being settled. "Nor shall any persons be deprived of life, liberty or property without due process of law": the resounding phrases of the Fifth Amendment are an echo of Magna Carta's Clause 39. In America as in England, Magna Carta became a potent symbol of men's struggle for freedom and human rights.'

Eight hundred years of it, in the foreground sometimes, at others in the background. Pitt the Elder described it as 'the Bible of the English Constitution'. Lord Denning called it 'the greatest constitutional document of all times – the foundation of the freedom of the individual against the arbitrary authority of the despot.'

The axis it created is still observably and obviously there. Anglo-American capitalism is a cultural/political as well as an economic phenomenon; we don't need to summon any mystical national spirit to propose that America and Britain share a view of liberty that is foreign to Continental Europe. Fascism and communism – systems where citizens owe everything to the state – have never flourished in Britain. And the origins of this attitude are there in the old charter.

'No constable or any other of our bailiffs shall take any man's corn or any other chattels unless he pays cash for them ...'

'Henceforth, no bailiff shall put anyone on trial by his own unsupported allegation, without bringing credible witnesses to the charge.'

'... the English church shall be free, and the men in our realm shall have and hold all the aforesaid liberties, rights and concessions, well and peacefully, freely and quietly, fully and completely for them and their heirs of us and our heirs in all things and places forever ...'

These freedoms, the right to trial, the presumption of innocence, *habeas corpus*, the rights of the individual against the state, these qualities (or, in Blair-speak, *values*) show the living vigour of tradition.

The French political culture was founded on very different values. King Louis said: *'L'état, c'est moi'*; they cut off the king's head and formed a revolutionary government headed by Robespierre, who showed how powerful tradition is by saying that the people had a single will and that he himself was the people. In the end, they had got rid of a king only to find themselves with an emperor.

The Code Napoleon – so very different from the Magna Carta in principle and in effect – still animates the French political culture. But it should be remembered that the proscriptive, *dirigiste* Code was imposed on a number of colonies – eight out of ten of which are still the poorest countries in the world. This is almost certainly not a coincidence.

During the Concorde project, a French official was asked whether the government had consulted local residents underneath in the areas affected by the plane's sonic boom. He was a man in whom the culture vibrated. He said, 'Of course not. When draining a swamp you don't consult the frogs.'

That is the French way of doing things. Why should it sound so scandalous to propose there be a very different way of doing things that is British?